SurvIved

My Life Story

by

Deneatrice Ledbetter

ISBN-978-1-960853-06-6

Liberation's Publishing LLC
West Point - Mississippi

In chess the most important piece on the board is the King but the queen is the most powerful

--Charles & Laura.

Table of Content

Sharing your story isn't a sign of weakness, it shows strength. Your story may be the very one that saves someone.

--Deneatrice

Chapter *One*

Trenton, New Jersey was so cold. I remember being a little girl walking to school with my mom every day. She didn't want me riding the bus because I was only in kindergarten. Dad drove the one car we had, because he worked on a base in Fort Dix. She and I would walk hand and hand across the railroad tracks to school. My teacher was Ms. Brown, and she had this beautiful white hair that she kept cut low. This particular year was her last year of teaching. She would be retiring. There were only two black kids in her class, and I was one of them. I always felt uncomfortable because of my natural hair. I was so tender headed that my mom only did the bare minimum to it because of me crying so much.

Like I mentioned, it was so cold in Trenton, and one day while at home watching the snow fall, I saw how beautiful the mountains were across the street from our townhouse. I asked my dad could he take me up the mountain one day. He did, and when he did, it was amazing, very cold, but amazing. So here we go up the mountain bundled tight. I remember midway up, I started to get scared. My dad laughed and said, "Why are you looking like that? Do you think we're going to roll back down the mountain?"

"Yea!" I replied. I was thinking that the entire time we were climbing the mountain. I wanted us to turn around and go back, but he kept going.

My dad was adventurous. He wasn't scared of anything, and he was mean as a pit bull. I am every bit of his attitude, demeanor, and drive. Someone was always telling me how great my dad was. They would also show me newspaper clippings of how great he was at basketball and baseball. He was great at track too, he could run. He was born Charles Edward Ledbetter AKA Doc, and was born February 3, 1952, in Columbus Mississippi. His parents were Rosie Lee Ledbetter and Edward Sanders. Dad was this strong man with zero tolerance for anything, a temper out of this world. A family man and a lady's man, a smooth talker. You know that generation. I'm so much like my dad, and I guess that's why we didn't get alone during my teenage years.

He received a full scholarship to Rust College in Holly Spring Mississippi, before he decided to enlist in the United States Army. While enlisted he served over thirteen years in the service before he received an honorable discharge. He received many awards while he was enlisted. After leaving the Army he moved back to Columbus, Mississippi and became the City Inspector there.

My cousins used to argue amongst themselves about who was my dad's favorite. When my cousin Toya was around, she was the favorite. When Stephanie was around, she was the favorite. When Nita was around, it was her. It was the same way for my baby sister and me. When I was around, I was the favorite and when my sister was around, she was. Everyone loved themselves some Charles. They knew him too. They knew he had a lot of women back in the day, and a mean streak. That mean streak of his he managed to pass down to me.

My mother, Laura Alice Williams-Ledbetter was born November 17, 1955, in Brooksville Mississippi. Her parents were Ora Bell Williams and Mr. Williams. She was a Noxubee High graduate and was mostly a stay-at-home mom who eventually started working at Sanders Plumbing. Eventually she took sick and was unable to work. Mom was the most beautiful woman you could have ever laid eyes on. She was very soft spoken but could get mean if you mad her mad. She loved her children and her grandchildren. Her hobby was watching her grandchildren play sports. Family was always first for her. She was the traditional submissive woman, no drinking, smoking, or clubbing. I brag on her all the time; she is such a good woman. She would help anyone, even if she did fuss and cussing, lol. Saying that she was strong is an understatement. She had the courage of a lion and fought like a bear. My real-life hero.

Dad told me the story of how he and my mom met. I never really believed him, but every single time he told the story it was the same. My mom was staying with her sister Mary in Columbus, Mississippi. Their family home had caught fire. Since the house caught on fire my grandmother Ora Bell had my mom move to Columbus, Mississippi with her oldest sister Mary Cockell until the family home was ready to move back into. On this day while staying with Mary, she went to the park and my dad was there. He was playing baseball and started showing out in front of her, because she was an unfamiliar face sitting in the bleachers. When he finished playing ball, he went over to her and asked her name. She replied,

"Laura."

"I'm Charles. Where are you from?" He asked.

"Brooksville, Mississippi." She replied awestruck from the door.

"I'm from here, Columbus." Dad said and then asked, "How does Laura Ledbetter sound?"

Mom fainted.

I would cry from laughing every time he told us that story. Mom's response was always, "He a damn lie!" But she never told us the "real story" as she called it.

A few weeks after meeting dad went off to basic training. They wrote each other letters back and forth. When he came home from basic training, he asked to marry her. They had only known each other three months, but they knew they loved each other. They got married March 1, 1974, in Reverend Hail's yard on Southside in Columbus Mississippi. Two years later, I came. I was born on the army base in Columbus, Georgia at Fort Benning. My first three years were spent there, and then we moved to New Jersey.

I remember it was my birthday. My mom and dad were good friends with our neighbors. They didn't have any children at the time, so they were like my second set of parents. They came over to the birthday party my mom put together for me. It was only cake and ice cream. One of the neighborhood kids came and celebrated with me as well as some other family members. Everyone gave me gifts and sang happy birthday. Later that night, I slept in bed with my parents because the family that came down to visit slept in my room. It was only a two-bedroom townhouse. I remember my mom telling me to turn over to the wall and go to sleep.

Our sleeping situation was like this, my dad was on the outside of the bed. I was on the other and mom was in the middle. Later that night when my dad thought I had falling asleep, he and mom started kissing which led to them having sex. For some reason I cried until they were done. I think my soul knew something was being deposited in my spirit. I woke up the next morning upset and quiet. I'm not sure what emotion this was or why I felt this way. Mom asked if anything was wrong, but I just said I didn't feel well. She let me stay home from school that day and things went back to normal, so I thought.

One Saturday morning, I was in my room playing with my toys. I got curious when thinking back to the night my mom and dad had sex while I was in bed with them. My curiosity led me to getting a pillow off my bed, going into my closet, and hunching it. It felt so good I thought. I heard my mom calling my name asking where I was. I froze and got incredibly quiet. She opened the closet door and there I was with my pants down and the pillow between my legs. That's the FIRST beating I remember as a child. Every chance I got I snuck into my closet with my pillow. I laugh at it now because this is where it all started. The introduction to heightened sexual desires at a young age. This followed me into adult life where you could say I was addicted to sex.

One day my parents went out to a party, and I had to stay with their friends who were also our neighbors. My second set of parents.

Mark would scare me so bad! He would dress up in different outfits just to scare me. I was so terrified of him. When my mom picked me up that night, I ran up to her and hugged her so tight. She asked me what was wrong, and I just started crying. My mom thought he had done something to me sexually, so she told my dad how terrified I was of him. I don't know if that was a good idea or not. But my dad went and confronted him. I never saw him or his wife ever again after that. I overheard my mom telling a friend in our kitchen one day that my dad had beat him so bad that she thought he had killed him. He never sexually assaulted me, only sacred me.

Time passed and mom was pregnant again. When she was nine months pregnant, I remember her screaming from the bathroom, "Charles! My water just broke." My dad took me next door to another set of neighbors. Her house smelled old, and her cooking was horrible. I stayed there two days before my mom came and got me. This was after she left the hospital with my first baby sister Monique Latrell. She was born November 3, 1980. She was so beautiful with hair all over her face. She looked just like a doll. My mom told me to sit back on the couch so I could hold her. She was so little. I asked my mom,

"Why does she have all that hair on her face like that?"

"Rich blood." Mom replied.

I had no idea at the time what that meant, so I just smiled and gave my little sister a kiss.

Time passed and my dad was stationed in Fort Carson, and it was cold too. Our apartment overlooked the beautiful city. Looking out of our living room window all I could see were beautiful lights. Our apartment sat on a hill, so we could basically see over the city. The view was amazing. One New Years Eve we were in the living room watching the count down on TV. Mom started counting, "ten, nine, eight, seven, six, five, four, three, two, one. Happy New Year!!" It was so exciting.

I went to school for a little too. My sister was growing, and she took her first steps the summer of 1981. She would walk around the house pulling everything down. My mom seemed happier, and that made me happy. We would go for walks in the park and visit a friend she had made while we lived there. Her friend's kids were older than us, so we didn't really play with them.

Things made a turn for the bad. One night I heard my mom in the living room crying. She was saying, "I'm so tired of this shit. I'm moving back home." I asked her where home was. She said, "MISSISSIPPI!" That was my FIRST time ever hearing the word MISSISSIPPI. I was born in Columbus Georgia at Fort Benning. That's where my father was stationed when I was born. What I later learned was my dad started using drugs, dealing with a lot of different women, and my mom was fed up with it. My dad was the primary source of our family's income, so my mom put up with a lot from him.

My dad got an honorable discharge, due to a knee injury, and they decided that we should move back to Mississippi. We had often visited Mississippi in the summertime, but this time we were there to stay. We moved in with my grandmother, my dad's mom, at first for a few weeks. Later we moved in with another family member. Here each side of the house had two bedrooms, we all shared a bathroom, and the kitchen. There was a total of four adults and four children staying in that house. Our back door, which was in the kitchen, didn't have steps to go outside. The house sat up high on bricks, so it was off the ground. One day I decided to jump down from that backdoor to the ground. I bruised my knee and fractured my arm; my mom was furious. But I was a dare devil and once I healed I did it again, and again. We lived there for a few years.

We finally moved out of the family home to a duplex apartment which was one bedroom. We turned the washroom into a bedroom for me and my sister. It was small, but it felt like home. The living conditions were much better, much cleaner and a safer environment. The property owner, though, was a bitch!

She had this wet jerry curl that was always dripping on her clothes whenever you saw her. She was our church member but was a very low-down woman who made my skin crawl. She would tell me every little thing my sister and I did. Vindictive, heartless, she was mean to us for no reason at all. Her house was next door to the duplex and one night we were outside in the street playing. My sister picked up rocks and started throwing them at her windows. She ran out of the house with her cigarette hanging out of her mouth and calling 911. The police came and she singled me out saying I did it. My dad gave me the SECOND worst whipping of my life behind that. I wasn't the one who did it. It was my sister Monique, but I took the punishment for it.

Time passed by and mom was pregnant again with my baby sister. Things between her and dad must have gotten worse without me realizing it. This particular day, she was nine months pregnant, and was in search of my dad. A friend of hers at the time, told her about my dad and this woman messing around and that they did it at the old family home. We went to the old family home and sure enough his car was parked there. Mom had me by the hand. (I don't remember where Monique was at this time.) We walked in and my dad and his lady friend were laid up in the bed sleep and naked! Still holding me by the hand she went into the kitchen and grabbed a knife. They never budged. They were still sleep when she went back into the bedroom and tried to stab the woman. My dad woke up and grabbed mom by the wrist she had the knife in and pushed her to the floor.

That push put my mom in labor. I was crying and screaming at my dad, "Why did you push her?" I would always think and, say to myself, "My dad defended the other woman and not his wife and unborn child." I helped her off the floor and we went home. She cleaned up and went to the hospital. That's when my third sister was born on August 7, 1982. Her name was Narquita Chiffon, and she was a big juicy baby with beautiful coal black curly hair. She looked like an Indian she was so beautiful, and a big crybaby, lol.

Deneatrice Ledbetter

Chapter Two

Christmas mornings we would all gather at my Grandma Rose's house. We couldn't open Christmas presents until we left church. We all would put on our nice dresses, suits, and coats, and walk to Zion Gate Church to have sunrise service. The Pastor would preach, and afterwards we would fellowship in the multiple purpose room and eat a great breakfast. After we were done with fellowshipping, we would walk back to my grandma's house and open our gifts. We would be in the living room, taking pictures, showing off our presents to each other. The times we had at grandmother's house were priceless. We would gather there for many different occasions. Basically, all holidays for the most part.

My cousin Deirdre was like my best friend. We would dress alike and go skating, to the movies, and other fun places. She was like my sidekick; I couldn't do anything without her. As long as I had her with me, my grandma would let me do anything. My cousin and I stayed at grandma's house quite a few summers. I had another cousin who treated me differently than the other cousins. Even though I looked at her as an aunt, and always respected her, no matter what. I remember one time; I couldn't have been more than eleven or twelve. She hurt my feelings so bad. Our cousins wanted something to drink, but she gave everyone cool aid except me. She gave me water. It doesn't seem like a big deal now, but as a child it hurt. I didn't understand at the time why she did it. She would make me take naps while the others were able to play.

When a child feels unloved, they will always remember. I will never forget those moments. When I got older, anytime I heard her name, or if I saw her, I would get angry all over again. As I got older things started to add up. A lot of it had to do with my dad. I always thought "why did she have to treat me badly because of what my dad did." As a child you will never forget how a person treats you.

My mom always took my sisters and me to the country in the summertime because of her work schedule. We went to stay with our grandmother who was her mother. We would stay the entire summer until we got of age to keep ourselves. Summertime 1984 came, my cousin Lisha and I were riding through the pasture on the outside of her dad's truck. I fell off and was hurt. I started screaming to my cousin that I had fallen off and for them to come back to get me. When my uncle backed up, I was still on the ground. He couldn't see exactly where I was, so he accidentally ran over my right leg.

My uncle picked me up, put me in the truck and drove me to grandma's so I could get into bed. That night I was in so much pain. The next day my leg was swollen so big, and it seemed like it didn't belong to me, it seemed disconnect from my body by the way it was hanging. My grandmother put me in the bathtub and rubbed my leg down with alcohol. That was what the old folks would do back in the day. They felt alcohol cured everything. My temperature started rising so, my grandmother called my mom and said, "You need to come gets her and take her to the doctor because something is wrong." My mother came the next day. So, I was lying in bed for two full days before I went to the doctor.

Once at the doctor's they rushed me straight back because of my temperature. They then did x-rays and ran tests. My leg was broken. I had to wear a regular cast for three months and a walking cast for another three months, half a year of my life with one functioning leg. I was devastated. My regular clothes didn't fit, but my favorite aunt Linda had some clothes that had wide legs that I could wear. I was ashamed of them at first because the kids used to laugh at me because they were bell bottoms. On top of that I had to ride the small handicap bus to school, because I was in a wheelchair. They would pick me up in front of my house every day and drop me right at the front doors of my school, Sales Elementary.

Ms. Bastrum, my teacher, was overly sensitive to my situation and made me feel comfortable as possible. Even when the kids teased me, she would punish them, by taking their recess or making them write sentences. After a long six months my cast finally came off. My legs were so little, black, and very dirty. It was so hard for me to learn how to walk normally again. I was scared to step my foot on the ground thinking I would break it again.

Vacation Bible school was the best part of the summer for us. I think I liked the snacks they gave us afterward most of all, they were what we all were waiting for. I met some good people while attending church there. It was mandatory that we went to Sunday School every Sunday to be able to attend Vacation Bible School. We didn't miss church even if we were sick. Honestly, we didn't even get sick back then. After Sunday School we had church service. It started at eleven o'clock in the morning sharp.

We had a children's Church choir. Me and my two sisters were in the choir. There was this one song we sang twice a month, and I always led it. My sister Monique had a voice out of this world, she was the soloist to the song,

We walk in the light ...
beautiful light ...
shine all around me ...
by day and by night ...
JESUS the light of the world.

The church would light up when she sang. That was one of my favorites. Everyone would ask her to sing everywhere we went. We didn't know where she got that voice from. She would sing in school plays at Mitchell Memorial School.

We all attended Mitchell, on Southside. It was one of the best schools ever. Mr. Brooks was the principal at the time. I used to be so bad, Ms. Brooks would beat the shit out of me with that paddle. Then when I got home my dad would beat me more. I was a talker, never would shut up. And I was the class clown of course.

Ms. Chism was our music teacher. I absolutely loved that woman she was sweet as pie. She had so many high hopes for me. She even let me lead a song in a school recital in the fifth grade. She knew damn well I couldn't hit those high notes, with this deep voice I got. I practiced for weeks, at school and home. The day of the recital, I was nervous. I had on a purple and pink dress, with some black flat shoes. My hair was in a side ponytail, and I had so much Vaseline on my lips you could fry chicken. I got up to grab the mic, took a deep breath, and started my solo. I was scared. I looked at Ms. Chism the entire time; she was lip singing with me. That woman made me feel like I could do anything I put my mind to do. I finished my solo and the crowd cheered. I felt like I had won the biggest prize ever. Honestly, I sounded like crap in my thoughts. But, hey if they were happy, I was too lol.

Mrs. Prince was my fifth-grade teacher and one of my best teachers. She was so nice, and considerate. She had high hopes for me too. She always encouraged me and told me I could be whatever I wanted to be in life, at that time it was a singer. That dream ended quickly. A few years later it was a schoolteacher.

During my seventh-grade year, my friends and I tried out for the cheerleading squad. We all decided on the outfit and socks we would wear for try-outs. It was a black tee shirt, turquoise shorts with a tutu attached to it, black socks, and white catfishes. We were poor and my mom couldn't afford to buy me the outfit we planned out. So, my cousin who was more like an aunt to me got some fabric and sewed me some shorts that kind of looked like my friends' outfits. My mom found me an old black tee-shirt of hers that was basically too big for me and some faded black socks I had had for a while. I had some catfishs already, so I cleaned them as good as I could.

We had the try outs and I wasn't chosen. I went to the bathroom and cried my eyes out. One of the teachers (who was one of the judges) asked me why I was crying, and I told her because didn't make the squad. She told me the reason I didn't make the squad was because my outfit wasn't like the others. And, if my outfit was like theirs, I would have made the team. She was one of the judges. At that very moment at the age of twelve I knew that I would grow up different. I had a mindset that I would NEVER be poor once I grew up.

We lived in a house on fifth street that I absolutely hated. It had two bedrooms, my parent's room, and my three sisters and I shared the other room. The rent was only seventy-five dollars. When we first moved into the house, us girls had one queen sized bed that we slept in together. We were so little at that time that it wasn't hard for us to sleep together comfortably.

My best friend Dionne lived right across the street from us. We did everything together. I would always tell a lie like my grandmother's house down the street was my house. Once we were at a summer church convention and we had to walk from my church, which was Zion Gate, to the church on tenth street. I always loved the summer conventions we had. We had to pass my house on the way to the other church. I remember my sister and some of my other friends, Kanesha, Nikki, and others, standing on our porch as I walked by with Dionne. I was so embarrassed when they called my name. I tried to ignore them. One guy yelled out, "Dee those little girls calling your name." The house we lived in was so old, and I was so ashamed of it.

Things with my parents were still bad. When I got home that day, I told my mom that I had to go back to church later on that night. We were having another program. My mom said "OK."

My dad yelled and said, "You can't go. I got something to do tonight, and you got to watch your sisters."

My mom then said, "I said she can go."

My dad rushed into the room where my mom was. She was hanging up a picture on the wall. He slapped her in the face and said, "I said she cat go!"

That was the first time I ever seen my dad hit my mom. They always fussed but he never hit her. My mom then pushed my dad so hard he went into a dresser. He was in disbelief at her strength. My dad never once again struck my mom ever from that day forward. My mom was telling me I could go because she was off that day. She usually worked from three in the afternoon until eleven at night. That's why dad was saying I couldn't go. He didn't know she could keep my sisters herself.

Deneatrice Ledbetter

Chapter *Three*

One morning I woke up and felt wet. I went into the bathroom and looked in my panties and there was blood. I was twelve at the time. I told my mom and she said, "Go get a pad off my dresser."

I was looking like, "What? What is this? What's going on?"

My mom said it again, "Go get a pad off my dresser."

I went and got the pad like she asked, and I put it in my panties, still confused. Neither my mom nor dad told us about the birds and the bees, nor did they explain how our bodies would change with time. I basically learned it on my own. My cycle used to be so heavy I would leak through my clothes at school. My mom took me to the doctor to see why I was running so heavy. It was so bad that I had an excuse from the doctors to stay home the first two days of my monthly.

My mom would get up early on Saturday morning to go to garage sales and buy our clothes. People thought we had money because of the way my mom dressed us. There were three things my mom mastered that I felt no one in the world could do better than her. One was ironing clothes. People at school and church thought we put our clothes in the dry cleaner's. The second was that she could slick our hair so good with gel and make it lay down no matter how bad of a hair day we were having. Last but not least the absolute best thing she did was fry chicken. She was the best on the face of this earth. That woman know she could fry some chicken.

Income tax was our time each year. We would get new clothes and shoes, and we would go to the "ten cents store" as we called it back then, and get nail polish, and jewelry. We didn't get much for Christmas but, tax time we splurged lol.

New Years Even 1989 my mom went out with a few of her friends. My mom never went out, all she did was church and home for the most part. When she came home from her night out, she put on her nightgown, turned on some music, and told us to come dance. We held hands and danced to Keith Sweat. I remembered so clearly. My mom was smiling while we were holding hands and dancing. It was something I had never experienced with her before. I was hoping that moment would never end. My sisters were so little but the smiles on their faces were priceless. The next day was the New year. We went to church. Mom cooked a good meal, we ate, and watched tv in the living room as a family.

My best friend at that time was Dionne, and we would play up and down the hill that was in front of our house. In my yard we had this big ole tree, I would climb up in it, and scare kids when they walked down the hill. Dionne would scare kids with me sometimes. She and I wanted to become rappers, lol. We wrote a rap down on paper, and she rapped it best. I still remember all the words. She would say, "Dee bust a beat." I would bust a beat then, she would start her part,

My name is lady De I'm telling you girl,
I'm rapping this beat, it's out of this world,

I'm rapping it nice, I rapping it good,

I'm rapping it like a young girl should.

We thought we were going to be famous after that. They called her De also, mine was spelled Dee, and hers were spelled De. I always remembered her birthday, May first. Her family, Tippy, her mom, Hoppy and Grandma Jennings introduced me to "8th of May". Down in the country they would beat drums and have a good ole time. I loved and looked forward to it every year. Her parents treated me like their own. Grandma Jennings would feed us and watch my sisters and me from time to time.

I remember once there was a big party at a club in Sandfield. It was Teen night. I knew my dad would not let me go. So, Dionne and I fooled my dad like she was having a sleep over at her house. Well, I thought we fooled him. Anyway, that night I packed my bag as if I was going to her house across the street. My dad told me to come home as soon as I woke up the next morning. When we got to her house, we got ready, and her dad dropped us off. When we got to the club, we were able to have fun for a while. I was partying, having the time of my life. A guy I had a crush on was there. We talked for a minute before the girl he was liking at the time came in with a bad ass outfit on. She was naturally beautiful. So, he brushed me off. It didn't stop me from having a good time. He had previously told one of his friends that we both knew that I was too skinny. That's why he wouldn't talk to me. Now that same man until this day is in my inbox begging for a chance. I leave his ass on READ! He looks nothing like he did in school. Remember the saying, "back then you didn't want me know I'm hot THEY all on me" lol.

Just before the closed at eleven o'clock a fight broke out between some guys. We all started running out, and ducking because they were throwing beer bottles, chairs, and anything else they could find to throw. We finally got out of the door, and everyone was running around everywhere. I looked in traffic, and who did I see? My dad! I knew I had to come up with a lie and quick. I started crying, messed my hair up, and tried to wipe the lipstick I had on off. He didn't play that make-up stuff at my age, lol. I finally got up my nerves to run to the car. My two little sisters were in the backseat.

I was screaming, "Dad, they hit me in the head with a bottle." My dad looked at me dead in the face and said, "You going to wish they had killed you, because when I get home, I'm going to beat your ass so bad, you're going to wish you was dead." When I got home, the way he beat me I really wished I was dead. I grab the belt one, time and that really made him mad. He pushed me and I fell and hit the dresser. I thought that would make him stop, but only made him beat me worse.

My sister used to tell people how my dad beat me when we were coming up. They couldn't believe how strong I was to manage all those beatings. My dad used to beat me like I was a man. I was hit with everything and anything. I did stuff because I was so immune to the beatings. So, I just did whatever because I knew the outcome and was ready for the upcoming beatings.

Dionne's dad opened a club up down the street called the Pioneer Lounge. I used to work on the door for him some nights.

We also had a few parties there ourselves for teens, good ole times. The Sanders stayed next door to the club and across the street. We were always told they were our "kin folks" as the old people would say. We all stayed in a neighborhood where we all knew each other, and we could even go to bed at night with our doors unlocked without worries! We could walk in each other's houses and get sugar, milk, whatever we needed without even asking.

Nowadays social media would know before they even put the sugar in the cup that you borrowed some sugar. We wore each other's clothes and shoes. It was like everyone was a big ole family.

A big shocker came to me. One day at the bus stop one of the kids said, "Derrick is your brother." I ran home and told my mom what the kid had just told me. She confronted my dad, and he denied it like always. I looked at Derrick one day. It was on the bus, and I said to myself, "he looks just like my baby sister Narquita. I mean just alike." But no one ever talked about it. There were rumors, for years he was our brother. We rode the bus together and stayed down the streets from each other. I think my dad's side of the family knew the entire time honestly, well some of them. This is what people today call "Family Secrets."

Finally, I hit high school, Columbus Falcons. I gained some more friends who I considered real friends. Komawi and Sandra. If you see one of us, you see the others. I started liking boys in my eighth-grade year. I started liking this guy who wasn't in my school district, and we started kicking it. He was older than me, a lot older. I met him in high school Saturday detention. This detention was for anyone who did something in school and didn't serve in school suspension for it. You had an option to go to Saturday detention. It was held at his high school in their cafeteria. It was four hours long, eight in the morning until twelve noon. Both schools would come there to do their detention time. He approached me, licking his lips just like guys do when they are lubricating their lips to tell lies. He asked me where I was from, and did I have a boyfriend. I said, "no I don't, you must want to be." From that we started dating.

I was really into him, he was handsome, strong, and popular. We talked for a few months on the phone. We only had landline phones back then. One day I skipped school to spend some time with him. He didn't pressure me at all to have sex. We kissed and touched each other but that was about it. My dad found out I had skipped school and beat me senseless. I was a problem child around that age. Always getting in trouble at school, being the class clown, smart mouth, talking back to teachers you name it.

A few weeks after my skipping school incident, my sisters and I came home from school, and my dad and some of his friends were there. My mom was at work at Sanderson Plumbing. We went into our room, and I tipped down the hallway to see what my dad and his friends were doing. I saw them open the stove up and realized that they were cooking cocaine in my mom's stove! I called the guard shack at my mom's job and told them to tell her to call home as soon as possible. The guard told me to hold on and he went to get her. I told my mom they were in the kitchen cooking dope in her stove. My mom immediately rushed home. She went off on my dad and made all his guests leave our home. My mom went back to work and once again, my dad beat me for telling on him this time. This is how I found out how bad my dad's drug problem was.

My mom worked from three in the afternoon until eleven at night, so she was at work most of our waking time at home. My dad and his friends would be in our living room getting high. It got so bad that he started pawning our things just to get high.

Deneatrice Ledbetter

Chapter *Four*

My sister Monique was a singer, and a dancer, while my baby sister Narquita only danced. We had an uncle called SNAKE and he had a group called 'Snake Brakers." Well, that's what I called them, lol. He would host talent shows at the old Princess theater. My sister secured an agent. He saw them perform at the Princess Theater in downtown Columbus. It was on fifth street right across from Fred's Dollar store. He approached them one night and asked them did they had a manager. At the time uncle Snake "Sanders Weatherby" was training them basically. They were the Snake Breakers lol. Anyway, he talked with them and started practicing with them, and showing them different moves. I couldn't dance, so I used to watch and laugh. They would be outside in the parking lot where we lived doing dance routines. He had both my sisters travel everywhere and compete in many competitions.

Monique had two friends that were at our home like they were our blood sisters. My mom loved them like her own. Shonda Faye practically lived with us. And Keona stayed in Oakdale Park, but she was over a lot also. They were like my little sisters. They all were some talented young girls. They were even academically smart. Monique was a good friend; she was the one that was the 'peacekeeper' unlike me and Kita we were "hell raisers."

I had a cousin, LaToya, and we were like sisters growing up in our younger years. She was my first best friend. Her mom Linda used to always tell me, "When Toya gets sick you the only one that can make her well." Toya and I had a bond that was unbreakable. Once we all lived at my grandmother's house together. I always made her, and her sisters laugh. When I would take my shower at night, I would be in the tub singing the Zest™ jingle.

Zestfully clean,

Zestfully clean,

you not fully clean unless you're zestfully clean.

I loved that commercial. I would come out of the bathroom, and her and her sisters Shawn and Stephanie would be so tickled at me. The killing part was we didn't even use zest soap. We had some type of off brand soap, and Tussy™ deodorant. I hated using that deodorant. I had to dig my fingers in the cream like deodorant to put it under my arms. It was cold and felt weird for the first few hours. Later, we started using the roll-on kind. It used to be the stuff back them. And, for toothpaste we use AIM™ in the white tube. It was thick and you got your money's worth because it was only a dollar.

My grandmother Rose used to make this tea like I had never tasted. Even today I've never tasted anything like it at all. I hate tea personally, but Her's I could drink a jug of it in a day. Her deviled eggs were my favorite. Anytime I had an event or just wanted some she would make them for me.

Southside was my stomping ground, and the projects were directly across the street from us. A few of my friends at the time stayed over there, Vicki and Queen. Next door to my grandmother's house was my Aunt Carrie's house. My friend Lakedra stayed there. She was older than me and taught me a lot. Billy's store was down the street from my grandma's house across from the cemetery. Emma's on fifth street had the biggest, juiciest burgers you could ever eat. She had once cent cookies that were big and round. I would look for pennies on the ground just to walk there to get some. When I had five pennies you couldn't tell me anything, lol.

We had the Jim Pippy store. I used to call it the hood store. We used to all hang out around it. Straight up fifth street led to downtown Columbus. We had Fred's, which was a discount store. Then there was Ruth's, which was a high-end store back then. My grandmother had a credit limit there. Ruth's sold all the Guess™ clothes and church attire. My grandmother was clean every Sunday with her matching hats. We also had the 10-cent store. My friend's and my favorite store.

One of my friends got in trouble one time for stealing some mood lipstick. Our lips used to be so shinny. Back then you didn't go to jail for stealing. They told your parents, and you would get a beat down.

The Varsity Twin movie theater was on the corner across from the Gilmore Inn. The things that used to go on in that movie theater. Afterwards straight to the hotel. We used to rent a room and throw pool parties. There were no guns, no fights, just fun. The drink back then was CYSCO™, the peach kind.

The Winter Circle was one of the hottest spots in the GTA. It was located on highway 82 east in the plaza where Winn Dixie grocery store was located. Thursday nights were considered College night. But all ages took over. I even stole my mom's Id to get into that club. The man at the door said, "this isn't you." I couldn't do nothing but laugh. I went right outside and found me an ID so I could get in. Back then you could be a child and buy cigarettes, but they wouldn't let you in the club at seventeen, lol. One time I got so drunk in the "Winter Circle." I was on that CYSCO. My child's father had to take me home and bathe me, I was so embarrassed. They used to say cocaine was in that liquor.

Church's Chicken was my mom's favorite. She loved their okra and chicken breasts. I guess that's why I like them so much. Southside, Columbus Mississippi is what made me.

The situation between my dad and I got worse. We were too much alike. My mom asked her sister if I could stay with her for a while because my dad and I weren't getting along. *I would babysit and clean her house for her on the weekends for extra money.* The way my dad was beating me scared my mom. She thought he would severely hurt me one day. My aunt agreed and I moved in with her. A few months had passed, and things started looking good for me. I was doing better in school, my grades were going up, and my behavior was much better.

The guy I was dating from the high school across town, told one of my friends that he was going to break up with me. We had been talking for months and I hadn't had sex with him yet. She slept with him behind my back because she liked him too. I found that out later. I had been over to his house a few times after school because my aunt didn't get off until late and my uncle didn't care. As long as I made it home before her, I was good. One Friday evening after lunch my friend and I skipped school for the rest of the day. I paged my boyfriend, and he paged me back.

Our code was 304, and it meant "it was finally going down." In a beeper if you turned the beeper upside down it spelled HOE, that was what I was supposed to send if I was finally ready to end my virginity. We texted 911 when one of us was in trouble or in a bad space and couldn't talk. Those beepers were the truth. Mine was red see-through with multiple-colored lights. I called him on his home phone from my friend's house and told him I would be over.

It was exactly one minute after three in the afternoon, when I looked at his alarm clock while lying in his bed. He started kissing me and touching me. I pushed back his hands when he got to my "pocketbook" as I used to call it. He got frustrated a few times. He then told me, "If you not ready to do this just say it and go home."

I said, "I love you and I want to do this." I was not even a hundred pounds wet. When he started taking my clothes off, I covered my face in shame. I was so embarrassed of my skin and bones. He caressed every part of my body, and just when I thought he was about to stick it in he went to town. He licked and ate every piece of pussy I had down there. My body was overheated. He then slipped a condom on and slid it in me terribly slow. He took his time and made love to me at the age of fifteen.

When I got home that day I went straight to my room and went to sleep. My aunt panicked because she thought I had not made it home. She called my mom to see hadn't she seen me. I was shut up in the room knocked out. I overheard her on the phone talking with my mom and got up and told her I was in my room sleeping the entire time. She was relieved that I was ok. After, we had sex, I felt like I had to continue to keep him. I realized who I was. I'm worth the wait. Ladies always remember YOU ARE ENOUGH.

My life changed drastically, one Saturday morning when my aunt had to go to work for a few hours. She asked me to clean the entire house. She always asked me to do it, and she paid me good. I was cleaning the living room, and I felt my uncle looking at me. I was uncomfortable but brushed it off and kept cleaning. When I got to their bedroom, I took the sheets off the bed to wash them. I felt someone behind me, I jumped. He then grabbed me by my shoulders and asked if I would like to make any extra money. I said, "no." I was terrified. I always considered myself strong, even as a teenager, but I was terrified! He then started kissing me on my neck and put his hands down my shirt. I was pushing him off saying no, but he overpowered me. He raped me in his own wife's bed.

I got up crying and hurting because of the force he used. I then locked myself in the bathroom. I heard his truck crank up. Once I heard him pull off, I grabbed the house cordless phone and called my boyfriend. He asked if I could sneak out of the house that night and I said I could. Later that night around ten, I told my aunt I was going to bed early. We were all in the living room watching tv. I went into my room, locked the door, and waited until they went to bed. I crawled out of the window, walked down the street, and jumped into my friend's car who was waiting on me. When I got to my boyfriend's house, he wasn't there. I paged him, no reply. I ended up going back home to bed. Come to find out, the next day he was with my best friend AGAIN. I didn't know who to tell about what had happened. My boyfriend and best friend betrayed me once again on the worse day of my life.

I went home the following weekend to visit. I told my mom and dad I had something to tell them. We were sitting in the living room, and I told my parents what happened. My mom was furious, and said she believed me because he had made passes at her before. My dad looked me right in my face and told me I was lying, and that I wanted attention. I cried and asked him to believe me, but he didn't. Instead, he told me to go to my room. While in my room the phone rang. It was my aunt telling my mom that her husband found the screen was missing from the bedroom window I was sleeping in. My aunt automatically told my mom that I had to been sneaking out at night, and that she couldn't deal with that, and I needed to move back home. My mom never said a word to my aunt about what happened at that time. It got brushed under the rug and no one talked about it again, until much later.

Back at home things were the same. There was this time my mom had been calling around looking for my dad all day and night. She went to a few of his hangout spots and still couldn't find him. She got worried because he had been gone for over three days. She thought something had happened to him. She drove this gray hatchback Honda that she had just gotten with her taxes that year.

My dad was in her car, and she needed to go to work. That's why she was looking for him. He finally showed up, but with no car. He and my mom went back and forth about that car. My dad told my mom someone stole it. My mom went to the police department to file charges. Come to find out my dad had pawned my mom's car for drugs, to some drug dealers in Alabama.

Mom was so mad. She told him, "Get out and never come back." My dad would not leave at first. My mom had put his clothes in black trash bags many times, but when she did it this time, she meant it. He ended up moving in with his mother around the corner, and that's where he stayed. Once my dad left, I had more freedom. I could finally go out with my friends and not have to babysit my sisters. My mom had gone to the first shift, so she could be at home with us at night since my dad was gone. My mom wasn't strict at all. She basically lets us do whatever. Now that I look at it, I hated it, but it did make me who I am today. Things were different in our home when dad left. We had more, seemed like. We were living better and defiantly more comfortably.

It was my sophomore year in high school, and I was still up to the same things. I was partying, class clown, talking and joking all the time. I dumped my first boyfriend and found another guy, older this time. He was out of school. One night while at Fox Run apartments Dionne, Tremika and I saw this guy. All three of us made a bet on who would get him. It was a funny, friendly bet. To sum it all up I got the guy. We fooled around for about six or seven months. I had no idea that he had previously dated a friend of mine. The damage was done. We had words about him but nothing major. She did try seeing him again after she found out about the both of us.

I met him around December the previous year, and he was scheduled to leave for basic training that summer. During our time dating, I was also talking to another guy who was around my age. Needless to say, I ended up pregnant at sixteen. The night before he left and went to basic training, I enlightened him about the fact that I was expecting. He was just as shocked as I was. He asked me was I sure it was his. I got terribly upset and started cussing at him. I was sixteen and he was nineteen. He left and went off to basic training.

As the months passed my stomach grew bigger and bigger. I picked up about twenty pounds, but I was all stomach. My little girl was kicking me, moving often and I had a glow about myself. I still stayed in school during my pregnancy. It was my tenth-grade year. Some of my friends' parents didn't want me around, because I was pregnant, and that made me feel some type of way. But I smiled through it like I had no idea they didn't want me around.

The day finally came for me to deliver my baby girl. My due date was November 4, 1992, but she had other plans to come early. My water didn't break, so they had to break my water. It was the worst feeling ever. My blood pressure was through the roof. My friends and family members kept calling up to my room, so the nurses told my mom they were going to unplug it until after I had the baby. It was adding stress. My mom didn't leave out of my room, not once, even to eat. She stayed by my side. My dad came into the room when I was about six centimeters. He asked was I ok. I told him I was thirsty because all they would let me eat were ice chips. My dad went to the vending machine, and got me a coke, and that's why I love Coca Cola now.

He opened it and poured me some in my cup of ice chips. My mom started fussing and cussing. She went into the hallway, found a nurse, and told them what my dad did. I was so tickled and hurting all at the same time. My dad told the nurse that I was thirsty and hungry, and he wasn't about to let me starve! The nurse got security, and they made him wait in the waiting room until I had my baby. He was furious and left the hospital. I was in labor a total of twenty-six hours. The worst pain of my life thus far. At twenty-six minutes past two in the afternoon I delivered a beautiful baby girl, weighing six pounds and ten ounces, on October 26, 1992. I was sixteen. My classmate Tish named her for me, Ta'Dashea Sharday. She was the most spoiled little baby I had ever in life encountered. My parents, cousins, aunts, friends loved her as their own.

For the first two years of motherhood, I did it alone with the help of my mother. My child's father would send checks in the mail monthly to help with expenses. At this time, he had only seen her in pictures. He was station in California once out of basic training. He finally came home when she turned two-years-old. He came in and laid eyes on his daughter for the first time and cried. He said, "She is really mine! She looks just like me!" I said, "Did you THINK otherwise?" Rumors had spread around town that I was pregnant by another guy I used to talk to. I knew it was not true, so I never worried about it.

Dashea had the biggest, beautiful eyes, and perfect eyebrows. Everyone would always tell me how beautiful she was. She was a straight A student until she reached middle school. She became a cheerleader in Junior High School. She cheered until her twelfth-grade year.

I changed high schools after I was ready to go back to school, after having my daughter. February of 1993, I started attending West Lowndes High school. I was neighborhood friends with a girl named Tweedy. My mom would drop me off at her house in the morning to catch the bus since the school was out of my district. She helped me around school and introduced me to some of her friends there. This is when I met my very best friend, Wendy.

We did so much together. We used to walk from northside to southside every weekend. And, when our money was right, we got a cab to see our boyfriends, lol. We did everything together. We would even become pregnant at the same time. We had some good times. We danced to every song that came on the radio. I used to stay at her house. She would stay at mine. Some of her friends before me, turned into some of my friends. We all got along very well, for the most part.

I had a class with this tall, dark, and handsome guy. His skin was so smooth. He was athletic, basically an all-around student. He had a girlfriend but didn't tell me at first. Come to find out, he told the girl I was his cousin. When I found out I was tickled pink. He was an abusive boyfriend; we would fight all the time. One time he had some brass knuckles in a coat and swung the coat at me, cracking my ribs and knocking my elbow out of place. I was in the hospital for two days and my mom was furious. Honestly, I did provoke him, but it still didn't give him the right to do what he did. My mom explained that. But I was in love, so I thought. He felt like he hit me because he loved me.

A few years passed and I was pregnant again. I was eighteen with a three-year old. Some of my friends from my old high school were still my close friends, I introduced them to some guys from Artesia but actually went to school at West Lowndes. We have so many stories behind those guys.

May 31, 1995, at eleven minutes after five in the afternoon, Ka'Daryal Mona Shonta was born. She was my mom's second grandchild. She was six pounds even. Labor with her was a piece of cake, seven hours and she was here. Her nickname was Booty. Her dad came up with that name. Where he came up with that, I have no idea. I remember her dad's cousin, coming to the hospital, to see my baby saying she looked just like him. I was like, "Yea I know." I said it with a sad face because he hadn't been up there to see me or his first-born child.

The next day after her birth she stopped breathing. The nurses ran to get the doctor. Come to find out she had a needle sized hole in her heart along with asthma. She was on a breathing machine the first week of her life. They told me to go home but my baby had to stay. It was so stressful; my mom went back to work, and I was all alone at the hospital. I received a call while there with her. It was her grandmother and aunt on her dad's side. They knew that her dad and I were dating but had no idea I was pregnant and had had a baby! I had asked him numerous of times, did he tell his parents and he said he did. I found out he hadn't. They both jumped right in and started helping me out with her. His mom came to the hospital and would stay all through the day so that I could do things. She was released a week later to go home. I was so happy and relieved.

When she started school, she was a terrible child. My mom would always to tell me, "All the things you did as a child you going to get back." Behold, I was getting all of it from Booty. She was so bad that when she was in kindergarten, I had to pick her up at twelve o clock daily. The very first day of school I had her by the hand taking her into the classroom, she was crying saying she wanted to go back home with me. I finally got her to calm down to stay. As, I was leaving and waving goodbye, I messed up and said, 'bye Booty." Why did I say that. All the kids in the classroom said "BOOTY, Ill, that's nasty!" She was so upset that she ended up going back home with me.

The principal told me that the only way she would come back is if her behavior was up to par. So, here I was with a five-year-old that wasn't allowed to stay at school after twelve. She hated her nickname until she got into middle school. She was known as a bully from daycare until she reached the age of ten. She finally grew out of being so bad. It was a relief.

Deneatrice Ledbetter

Chapter *Five*

One day we got a call informing us to get to the daycare as soon as possible. Once we got there, we couldn't believe what we saw. My aunt Bernice was lying on the ground in a pool of blood. Her husband was laid out in the road with the paramedics working on him. He had shot my aunt in the back of the head, and when she hit the ground, he shot her again. Afterwards, he then turned the gun to himself. It was a rifle. He placed the gun under his chin and pulled the trigger. My mom was furious about them on the ground trying to save my uncle. Why were they on the ground trying to save him?" My aunt was already gone. They hadn't even covered up here body. She was just lying there. I was screaming, "Cover her up! Cover up her! Why just let her lay there like that?"

Eventually they then placed her lifeless body onto the stretcher, put her in the ambulance, and drove off. We followed behind in the car. I put the blinkers on and drove behind the ambulance to the hospital. When we made it. Many of my family members had already gathered. We received the news about her passing. My favorite aunt, who was like a second mom to me, was gone within the blink of an eye. I had two nephews who were now motherless because of a senseless act of jealousy. My aunt's husband was an out of control, angry, human being. He lived, and after he was released from the hospital. He was arrested for what he did but made a bond. When he got out, he came to visit my mom.

There was a knock at the door, mom answered, and it was HIM. He stood there with his mouth wired shut, trying to speak. He had some type of device attached to him. It talked for him, but you couldn't understand some of his words, not all of them. He was trying to explain to my mom what happened. He even had the nerve to try and convince my mom that he was justified in doing what he did. I was like really. My mom told me to keep quiet. For the first time that I could remember my mom went completely off. She asked him to never in his life speak a word to her. We never saw him again, other than in the news and newspapers. In one article I recall them saying, "It was crime of passion." From that moment on, I kept my guard updating anyone.

Chapter *Six*

It was summer and I was at a game in Artesia. I spotted this guy with a mouth full of gold. I was in a daze and gloating about how handsome he looked. I asked a friend who he was, and she told me his name was Chris Harris. "He's from Starkville MS, has money, and a lot of women." I laughed. My friend got in his ear and told him that I thought he was handsome.

He came over and said, "what's up?". I stood there frozen like a little kid, smiling my ass off. He was a little older, but I knew I had him. We started dating even though he had a girlfriend. So went back and forth between both my daughter dad and him. As a young girl, at that time, Chris showed me how a woman was supposed to treated. He wined and dined me. He dated me like a real man supposed to. He brought me nice things like gold chains and rings, and I absolutely loved jewelry. Gold being my favorite. Money was never a problem for him. He gave me money to help with my two children that weren't even his. I felt like I was the only girl in the world. He had a girlfriend, but I didn't care. He treated me right.

This went on for about a year or so. Until He got locked up and his girlfriend left him. I would go to Rankin County, and other satellites facilities to see him. We dated for about two years while he was locked up. Finally, I was the 'MAIN" girl! Finally, I got the man of my dreams. Shortly after that he asked me to marry him. I was the happiest girl in the world at that time. Even though he was locked up when he asked to marry me, he held up to his promise. We got married February 8, 1997, in Jackson Ms.

After we got married, we had a handsome son on July 29, 1998, at 9:37 A.M weighing 9lbs. 8oz. We named him Christopher Lashawn Harris Jr. I finally gained some weight while pregnant with him. It took three children for me to finally get some hips, lol.

I basically went through this pregnancy on my own. I worked and even went in labor at work. It was an easy pregnancy, but hard. Chris was locked back up once again. He was just obsessed with the fast, street money. I loved it too because I didn't want anything. We had it all, the money, cars, house, you name it, we were good. But him not being there for the appointments, kicks, heartburn, sleepless nights, and labor put me in depression.

I had an aunt, Nancy, who owned her own Childcare Center in West Point. I worked for her. Chris was nine days old; when she called me and asked, "Dee can you please come back to work? One of my workers quit and the other one had to be out for a while." I could barely walk. I was depressed, and low on money. I needed to go back to work. I told my aunt, "Ok, I'll be there Monday morning, only if I could bring my son." She agreed and I went to work that Monday.

I hadn't told my mom I was going back to work, but she had her suspicions. She didn't believe in getting out so soon after birth or washing your hair until your baby had turned six weeks old.

You may be asking, "How did I end up here? I was just being

treated like a lady. What changed, when, and how? A woman is supposed to be submissive, take care of the house, the kids, the man, work, and still look their best at all costs. We hold all the titles, but don't even get half of the credit, attention, affection or love we deserve. We must remain strong, cry in the shower, and show signs of strength through it all. At all times we must be a girl with a mind, a woman with an attitude, and a lady with class.

My husband was incarcerated throughout most of the marriage. He was one of the biggest drug dealers in the GTA. During one of his bouts in prison, I started seeing this guy, Ken. He was a well-known guy around town. We would party, have amazing sex, and travel back and forth to Birmingham almost every weekend. We didn't have a title, but no matter when one of us needed the other, we showed up. We had so much fun together. Magic City classics, strip clubs, charming hotels, restaurants, you name it, we did it. He had a live-in girlfriend, and I had a husband who was locked up. I never missed a visit with my husband while he was incarcerated, and he heard rumors about Ken and me, but I always denied them. We always claimed that we were just cool friends, but everyone knew better. And it was all about to come to a head one morning while coming home from one of our Alabama exploits. My husband had transitioned to house arrest, and we were on bad terms. I told him I was staying over at my mom's house to get some space and let to spend time with "him."

We had gone to Birmingham the day before to party at a strip club. He had given me an ecstasy pill, and I was so high. I stayed in the room while he was out partying. When he came back to the room that night, we had the best sex we had ever had since we had been fooling around. The next morning, we headed home. We gassed up and got breakfast. He asked me to drive back. because his license was suspended, so I was always the driver. I think that's why I absolutely hate driving now.

He was driving for some reason, and I was sleeping in the passenger seat. I heard him say "SHIT!"

I jumped up and said, "what?"

"The police got me!"

We pulled over. He was smoking a blunt, so the car smelled like weed. He put it out in the ashtray not, thinking clearly, I guess. I asked him "IS THERE ANYTHING IN THIS CAR?" I knew what he did.

"NO." was what he said to me.

I replied, "Ok." I thought we should be ok.

By that time the police were at the driver's side window, and all I kept thinking about was my husband and children back home.

The police asked, "Can I see you license?"

He said, "I do not have any license." I knew then we were in deep shit!

"Do you have any illegal substances in this car?" The policeman asked.

"I just have this blunt." He replied. The officer had already seen as well as smelled.

The officer called for back-up, and they asked "Whose care is this?

"Mine." I replied.

"Can we search your car?"

"Yes." I replied under the impression that there was NOTHING, but the blunt in my car.

The other officers arrived on the scene with a dog. They searched the car high and low for about ten minutes. I thought it was all clear until under my spare tire in the truck were drugs. They placed both of us under arrest and took us to jail. I was in a holding cell, for about two hours. The detectives took me into a room and tried everything in their power to get me to give him up. I told them I had no idea where the drugs came from, or that they were even in my car.

"We have been watching him, and if you don't tell us where he got the drugs from, you're going to do a lot of time. They were in your car. He's saying the drugs are yours, and he doesn't know where they came from."

Another detective said, "you are holding up for him and he saying the drugs are yours. You are stupid and will never see your kids again."

I said, "I know he didn't say that. Like I said I have no idea where those drugs came from." They put me back in the holding cell until the next morning. The next morning, they transferred me to another jail for booking.

I called my mom first and she was furious. She was crying and asking me all kinds of questions. "Why? You have a husband at home and children." All I could do was cry and say, "I'm sorry and I know I messed up." My mom called and told my husband. All the rumors finally came to light. All the lies my friend and I had told our mates finally caught up with us.

A few days later we went before the judge, and he set our bond at ONE MILLION DOLLARS apiece! Everyone in the court room was in disbelief. All of his children's moms were there, his mom and day. My mom and aunt were there in the courtroom.

I missed my children's Christmas and spent the new year behind bars. We sat in jail for thirty-one days before they reduced our bond. After I got home my marriage was on the rocks, but my husband did not leave my side. He gave me a hard time but stood by my side through it all. Things were different. I could tell the love was fading, and he eventually went back to jail. Things went downhill from there.

Chapter *Seven*

In 1996 my sister Monique was pregnant with her first child. On October 25, 1996, she gave birth to her first beautiful baby girl. She named her Shan'Qula Lasha Fulton. She was the third grandchild in the family. So far, we had all girls like my mom. Dashea, Booty, and Qula were more like sisters than cousins. She was pregnant again a few years later and my question to her was "What would you like to do for your birthday, since you full of baby for your sweet sixteen lol." That's what the older people used to say back in the days, "full of baby." She laughed liked she always did, and said "Dee, I'm going to work." (We both worked at Ryan's at the time.) I said you better leave Shan, Sha, with mama girl, and go enjoy yourself. Not those exact words but like that, it was many years ago. Monique didn't celebrate herself that year. *As the years pass, we celebrate her every single year with a thoughtful post, or we take people down memory lane with great memories of her.* Monique was the true definition of a go-getter. She was a person who put her children before anyone. She loved and adored them. She was unselfish, had a heart of gold, a giving person, a singer, dancer, secret keeper, and finally a secret keeper and stayed true to her friends.

Monique decided that she wanted to enlist in the Army. She was scheduled to leave in August 1998. She packed her bags and headed out. So, when I walked into mom's house, she was sitting on the floor. I was confused. "Why are you here?" I asked her. You're supposed to be in South Carolina at Fort Jackson for basic training." She burst into tears; my mom was sitting on the couch. She looked at me and told me they sent her back, because she was pregnant. When she arrived at Fort Jackson, they did blood work and found out she was pregnant. She had done all the necessary testing before she left, but it was obviously too early for a pregnancy to be detected at that time. I was furious, very upset, because I knew who she was pregnant by, and nothing would come of it except drama.

April 14, 1999, Tierra Mona' was born. When Monique brought her home from the hospital I told her, "I'm going to spoil that baby." She laughed and said, "yea right. You already have three children of you own." Monique had Tierra a few weeks early so we postponed the baby shower until after she came home from the hospital.

I had already been through so much from the age of twelve until then, but nothing could have prepared me for what I was about to be hit with. One of the most tragic things in my life was about to happen. It was Saturday, April 23, 1999. We had Monique a baby shower. Tierra was nine days old. Monique was good friends with a neighborhood friend named Gabe. He helped her with the baby shower and helped my mom out on the grill that evening. It was getting dark, and we were in the yard. So, people stopped by joining in the fun with us. Around ten-thirty that night my dad called my mom and said, "Laura gets all those people out of your yard." The current Mayor at the time, Mr. Smith, and my dad were good friends.

He had called my dad and told him he had seen we had a yard full and to break it up before trouble started. Mom and I told the crowd that they had to leave. They went to the vacant lot across the street which we called "Trash Alley." It looked like we were having a big party in my mom's yard and across the street.

During this time the gangs were bad, and it didn't help that my sister had her daughter by a guy from the Northside of town which was where Vice Lords gangbanged. We stayed on the Southside which was where The Gangsters resided. You very rarely saw the two sides mix. They both stayed on their side of town even though some were friends with each other and were from different gangs. It was around twelve fifteen in the morning and a pathfinder/rodeo was coming up sixth street. At first, we heard what we thought were gunshots, but it turned out to be rocks. Then before we knew it people were running; real gunshots were fired. A van with five or more guys, some I knew, were shooting guns toward our direction. My cousin was in the street shooting a gun towards the pathfinder. Monique was beside me and we were running toward mom's house.

All of a sudden, the gunshots stopped. I didn't' see Monique beside me and I started screaming "where are my sisters? Where are my sisters????" I turned around and my sister Monique was lying on the ground. My mom was standing in the doorway with a look on her face that I'll never forget. I knelt down beside Monique and started shaking her.

"Get up! Get up!" I shouted while shaking her, "what's wrong with you? Say something!" Her eyes were wide open. I was thinking to myself, "She is having a "set back' which is what the older people used to say when you got out too early after giving birth. I started screaming, "Call 911! Call 911!" By this time the police had made it on site. All of the neighbors had called the police once they heard the gunshots. A police officer and I started giving Monique CPR. I knew CPR because I was employed at my aunt Nancy's daycare, and it was a requirement. The male officer was giving chest compressions and I was doing mouth to mouth. A crowd of people were around us.

All of a sudden, I heard my dad's voice, but it sounded far away. He was screaming "Dee. Dee, Dee, not my baby Dee." His voice got closer and closer and closer while calling my name. I remembered once he reached me, people were holding him back, and would not let him get to us. That's when he realized it was Monique on the ground and not me. My dad had run from 507 15th Ave south, to 701 11th Ave south. About a half mile or so, bare footed to get to us. The ambulance finally came. I begged them to let me ride in the ambulance with my sister. They told me no and to just follow them to the hospital. I got terribly upset and asked, "why?" Then one of the EMTs on back told me its best if I drive my parents because they were in no shape to drive. He was right.

We got to the emergency room and pulled up at the same time as the ambulance. I was trailing them. When we walked in, there were so many people at the hospital that night. A nurse walked out and said, "The Ledbetter family please come into this room on the right side." The immediate family and a few close friends all gathered into the room sitting, waiting, talking, asking each other questions. I sat there in a daze because all I could see was Monique's face while lying on the ground. About twenty minutes later Dr. Manning came into the room. She looked me dead in the eyes, when I stood to my feet. Then suddenly, she said "I'm sorry there was nothing we could do." The lights went off and the room was extremely dark! Everyone was screaming, crying, falling out. Suddenly the lights came back on. This was the WORST day of my life!!!

Morning came and the sun was out, I was in Monique's bed at my mom's house. People were stopping by, dropping off money, cards, food, drinks etc. People came to pray for us and give their condolences. I remember two particular people coming to see me. We had bad blood against each other because of a boy back in high school. They came into the room where I was laying and said, "we are praying for you. Let us know if you need anything." I said, "Thank you." And they vanished. I questioned myself was it real or a dream a few days later, but it was real.

Everything else for the next few days I was unsure about. My aunt Linda came over to the house to get Monique kids, Shan'Qula and Tierra, to help give us some time to get things together. My mom was adamant about Pastor Boyd, doing the eulogy for Monique's funeral. He was away at a conference, so we had to wait until he was back in town to have the funeral. When he got back to town in the earlier part of the next week, he wanted to meet with my parents. I went too of course. He asked my parents, "why were you all out there that time of the night anyway. You all had no business out there."

All I smelled was blood. I got so mad. I had a temper like my dad. Why would you ask a mother and father who just lost their child that question instead of asking if they were okay. He could have asked, "Do you need anything from the church? Or said, "we and the church family will be praying for you." I walked out and my mom asked me where I was going. I just kept walking and walked back to the house. My mom's house was just down the street from the church.

Later, we were sitting at the kitchen table putting together the obituary. We were trying to make sure we had everyone on the obituary that was supposed to be there. Out of nowhere my dad says, "put my two son's names on there." Everyone paused and looked in shock. Dad continued to name his two sons, "Dereck and Chris." My mom was furious, I could see the hurt in her eyes when my dad said that. Not only did she just loose her child, the Pastor in around about way made her feel like it was her fault, and now her husband decides to confess and break the news of his two outside children. This was all done while mom was cooping with the death of his daughter's death. The nerve of wanting to add them to her obituary.

My dad never told us that they were our brothers until that moment. It was always rumored, but never truly reconciled, until that moment. My mom sucked it up like she always did and let their names be added. I, on the other hand, was pissed. And I made it known that I was pissed. People were always hurting my mom's feelings and that made me angry.

My parents didn't have the money to bury my sister. So, my dad went to two of his sisters to get the money to bury her. The agreement was that he and mom would pay it back when they could. There was a program in Jackson called crime victims. They reimburse you back when it's a violent crime. One of my aunts that helped pay for the funeral kept harassing my mother. One day my dad called and told me my mom was upset, because Sandra called her going off. I think he did it for a reason. If you knew my mom, you knew she had soft feelings. So, I went to my grandmother's house where my aunt was. And one thing led to another. I was two inches from knocking her into the wall, before my cousin, the one who was more like an aunt to me, called the police on me. I left and headed home. I saw the police pass right by me.

My cousin and aunt told them where I was staying and sent them to my house. I was smarter than that. I had gone to a friend's house. The crazy part about all that was my dad started all of that mess. He knew I was going to go off. When I pulled up, he left the house and went next door and told Pimp and Carrie to come get me before I got in trouble. The trouble he put me in. My dad was good at making sure I knew things, because he knew I had no filter, and I was coming, especially about my mom.

After the funeral my mom went downhill and went into depression. She would be in her room at night crying out asking why her baby had to leave her. For a while I felt like it was my fault. I felt like it was my problem to solve.

A broken heart can kill you and mom ended up getting sick. She found out she had congested heart failure, high blood pressure, and diabetes. She even had to leave her job because of her illnesses. She started receiving disability benefits. She kept getting worse and my grandmother, her mom, would come over and help out. She would come cook and clean for mom and help with Monique's children.

The headings in the news lines were "Teen-age mom killed in drive by shooting." In the article it sated that I said, "I lift her shirt halfway up to see if she was breathing." Columbus Dispatch even went as far as bringing up that my dad was a former City Housing Inspector who made newspaper headlines the year prior for pleading guilty to extortion, and that he was out on state probation. The local news station used my sister's death in their headline for months after her death. It had my mom so furious; she went up there and asked them to please stop giving the family constant reminders of the death of her child. They finally stopped, after my mom and dad got the mayor involved.

A little time passed and one day while working at my aunt Nancys daycare, my mom and grandmother came by to visit after leaving my mom's doctor appointment. They left to go back to Brooksville where my grandmother stayed. From there they were leaving and headed back to my mom's house in Columbus. They were getting off at the Columbus exit, when an eighteen-wheeler, drove passed them and the tire blew out on the truck. The blowout from the tire sent rubbish into the air and onto mom's windshield. She couldn't see the road clearly. She flipped the car into a ditch.

As, family gathered at the hospital we received the news that my grandmother did not make it. My mom came out without a scratch. We were later told that my grandmother possibly had a heart attack because the wreck scared her.

Today, we live in a world where we don't talk to our mother because of a simple disagreement. We feel like she loves our other sibling(s) more than she loves us. We don't have any dealings with their father because he wasn't in our life as a kid. We don't speak to our siblings because we had a small falling out or are jealous of one another. We don't talk/have a relationship with our uncles, aunts, nieces, and nephews because of generational curses. We don't talk to our cousin(s) we grew up with like brothers and sisters due to lies and greed. We don't talk to certain family members because they treat their spouse boyfriend, girlfriend, mate, family members more like family than their own. (Thinking that will keep that man/women) even though the family plays BOTH sides.

We discipline our children, and grandchildren for their wrong doings, and we teach them not to bully. Yet and STILL, we are teaching them otherwise by our actions we have against our OWN FLESH and BLOOD. It's time to release all the hate, drama, and start setting examples for our upcoming generation. Sometimes you don't know why, when or even what caused the distance. Just remember it all starts with YOU! Matching energy is why everyone is miserable, you can't clean dirt with dirt.

Chapter *Eight*

My husband eventually got out of prison and came home again, and we worked on our marriage. We bought our first house in Columbus. It had four bedrooms and two baths, a genuinely nice living area, with fireplace, and a nice size kitchen and dining area. We got all modern furniture to decorate the entire house.

I still worked, but ended up getting hurt while working, and was out awhile on leave. While off work I had time to think, I woke up one morning and told my husband that I wanted to open my own daycare one day. He told me to find out what the process was and how much the startup would be. I spoke with my aunt. She told me the ropes, the ins and outs, and the startup cost I needed to open. I went home and told my husband what I needed to get things rolling. He gave me twenty-five thousand dollars and a year to get it going. Within the first six months business was booming. I had a few family members children, a few old classmates, some teacher's children from the nearby high school, and friends.

For three years everything was finally coming together. Business was great, my marriage was good, kids had everything they needed and wanted. We were traveling more. Just living a good life. Then "Boom!" I got a call from my husband who was in the back of a police car. He said, "baby they got me again." He had gone through a roadblock in the truck I had just gotten for myself. He had substances in my truck. They impounded the truck and locked him up. He had no bond. I had to go get my truck out of the pound myself. Since he was a third time offender, he went away for a long time this time. I went into deep depression and started drinking heavily.

During this time, I met this guy who was a good friend. This time a good friend only. I told him I wanted to go to Jamaica for my birthday and he made it happened. He sent me on an all-expense paid vacation to Montego Bay Jamaica. Back then you did not need a passport to travel. All I needed was my birth certificate and ID. I went to Jamaica with a friend and had the best time of my life. We flew back into Atlanta, from Jamacia on a Tuesday. When the plane landed, we started getting our overhead baggage down from up top. The pilot came on the intercom and said, "everyone sits back down and, take your ID. Have them handy once you depart the plane." As we were getting off the plan there were about six policemen with guns, and riffles asking for my ID. Once I gave it to them, they slammed me onto the ground and told me that I had a warrant for my arrest.

I learned later that the charges that we had in Alabama weren't taken care of. The guy did the time was back home and everything, but my lawyer had messed up my paperwork. I was considered a fugitive in the state of Alabama. I was in disbelief and confused. I sat there for about a week. My husband had hired a lawyer to get me out, and the attorney set me up a new court date. I was released just like that and on my birthday. I was going home. I remember I had to catch a bus to Tuscaloosa, Alabama and my cousin Monika and my sister, Narquita came and picked me up from the bus stop.

That following weekend I had a party at club Legends, it was already in the making before I left and went on my trip. I am VERY BIG when it comes to my birthday even until this day. The DJ that I booked that night sucked. I was so mad. My mom and friends tried to calm me down, because he was not playing the kind of music I was requesting. By the end of the night, I was pissed and intoxicated. My mom was worried about me getting home safely. There was a guy there who had been after me for a while. He told my mom that we were really good friends, and that he would drive me home. He was a total gentleman. He made sure I got home safe, and into bed.

The next morning, I woke up and he was on my couch asleep. I asked him what he was doing there, *(I had forgotten about the night I had previously lol)* and from that moment we started dating. He was a rapper, out of my norm. I was used to drug dealers with fast money. But he was an overall good person. He also had a side hustle, selling CD'S and DVD" S on the side. I never knew him to ever have a job other than rapping lol. He was an impressive cook. He catered to me by being supportive, cooking, making sure the house was straight, helping with my children, and helping me pay bills. He even had my nieces and children rapping. He introduced gambling, which I already had it in me anyway from seeing my mom playing cards, when I was younger. That's when I met Drico. He was so young but had an old soul, I thought to myself, if you know what I mean. He carried himself differently from the guys his age. He was one of the funniest, messiest people you could ever meet. We would gamble and play cards, (playing cards) to over into the next day sometimes. After a while Drico became like a brother to me. We would hangout and party. At this time things were going good so, I thought. I was still married, but my husband was incarcerated. I had been through this already with him two times, and I could not do it anymore. He eventually found out about the guy I was dating. So, I stopped going to see him, and he started dating a girl he met while he was locked up. He went his way, and I went mine.

Chapter *Nine*

My friend Wendy and I were out riding one night, and we rode by a few clubs, and hot spots. We rode past a club called the GOOSE; I hated that club. It was ghetto, but it was a hot spot back then. As we were riding past, I saw the rapper. He was standing there in some girl's face, flirting like he always does. I asked Wendy to keep going. I called his phone, while looking at him as I passed by. He took the phone out of his pocket, looked at it, then put it back into his pocket, not even answering.

"OK, two can play this game." He was too busy entertaining the person he was talking to, to answer his phone. I told my friend let's just ride around. My plan was to waste enough time for him to make it home before I do. I wanted him to call my phone when he got home, so I wouldn't answer.

My planned worked he got home, and I wasn't there. He called numerous times, and I didn't answer on purpose. When I did make it home, I did what a person should never do when they come in late hadn't been answering their mate calls. I walked straight into the bathroom and cut the shower on. When I was bending over to check the temperature of the water, I felt something in the back of my head. I turned around immediately; it was a gun! I freaked out. I started screaming asking "why would you pull a gun out on me? My children and your children are in there sleeping. What are you doing?"

I saw the look in his eyes. He had been drinking heavily. I told him to get out. Leave now, you can come back in the morning when the kids wake up and get them, but you must leave now. He left the house. I laid down and must have dosed off. It couldn't have been any longer than thirty minutes or so after he left the house. I was awakened by him turning on the lights. I said, "cut that light off and why are you back here?"

He said, "I apologize, and I would never do anything to harm you."

I turned on my stomach and turned my head the opposite way. He kept saying, "Dee look! There's no bullets in this gun. This is the gun I got from ole boy. It won't shoot. Look!" All the while he is pointing the gun directly at me.

I shouted, "I said, DO NOT POINT THAT GUN AT ME AGAIN!"

He then pointed the gun at himself and continued insisting, "Dee, ain't no bull …"

"Boom!" He shot himself and hit the floor. He landed beside a basket of white clothes that I hadn't folded yet. He got up, grabbed some of the clothes out the basket, and used them to hold his face together. I went into shock and screamed.

The bullet went through under his chin, and the came out under his eye. He did it with a nine-millimeter gun that wasn't supposed to be working. I was still screaming, and he was trying to calm me down, while blood was dripping everywhere.

At this point my children and his children had woken up, but they did not know what was going on. He finally calmed me down and told me to take him to the hospital. He also told me to hide the gun. I was still in shock and couldn't move. He started screaming at me saying, "Dee! I'm a convicted felon. I can't get caught with this gun." I hid the gun. The detectives and the police tore up my house looking for that gun, but they never found it. It was right under their nose.

He had another gun, but he threw it out of the window as I was driving him to the hospital. He also told me what to tell the police if they asked what happened.

We got to the hospital in about three minutes. My house was in the same area. Once there, the people were looking at me in amazement. I did not understand why at first, then I looked down. All I had on was a tank and underwear, no shoes or anything. They gave me a hospital gown to put on and some of those surgery shoes. They immediately took him back and started to work on him.

It started to dawn on me what had just happened. The hospital was packed out by now, with his family, my family, and friends on both sides. The doctor came out and told me he had to undergo a very intense surgery and that it would take hours. Some of my family went to my house to get me some clothes. We were sitting in the ICU waiting room for hours awaiting the doctor to come back in with an update.

While waiting the detectives came in and asked to speak with me. They took me back into a room of the hospital and asked me what happened. I froze and broke down crying. Then one detective asked me, "Did you shoot him?"

"No!" I immediately said. "I'll take a lie detector test if you would like." *Too many Lifetime movies.*

They said, "no, you don't have to; we just want to know what happened."

I told the story the way he asked me to. Once I finished the detective that was talking the most said, "You are lying." They then asked me can they dust me for gun powder residue. I immediately said, "Yes," and they did. They then went on to say, "we know you did not do it because of the evidence we found in your home."

I thought they had found the gun, but that wasn't it. They found the bullet hole and shell casing. They then released me as a suspect and asked me what happened. I told them the truth, then they closed the case. Everything they told me, lined up with their findings. I went back to the ICU waiting room, to join back with my family and friends. Everyone was asking the same questions, "what happened?" Did you, do it? Did someone else do it?" I sat there in silence. After a while the doctor and a nurse came in. They asked which one of us was Dee. I respond that it was me. The doctor then goes on to say he's stable but had a long recovery ahead due to some other issues. He only wants you to come back, no one else. When I walked into the hospital room, I was looking at a miracle lying in that hospital bed. His mouth was wired shut. He was under a lot of medication, but they gave him a clipboard and pen to write what he needed to say.

"Are you okay?" he wrote.

"No," I replied.

"I'm sorry."

I started to cry.

I went to every visitation he had. His sister set it up so that only she and I could go back to see him. When he was ready others would be able to go back.

At this time, my business which was my daycare center took a huge hit. Parents were concerned about the wellbeing of their children. The rumors got out of hand. Everyone was going around saying that I did it. The biggest rumor was he was beating me, so I shot him. You name it, they produced it. I had a parents' meeting letting all the parents know what was going on and that I had absolutely nothing to do with his gunshot wound. This meeting along with help from my mom and cousin, Perlisha. Things picked up again.

He was finally released from the hospital. His mouth was wired shut, so he had to drink protein shakes, and ensure, because he couldn't eat normal food. I was frustrated. He was frustrated. Running my daycare on top of this was just too much. We decided that it was best if he went to Chicago for a while, until he got better and was able to get the wires removed. He eventually did get better and came back.

We ended up leaving that house because I could not sleep in my bedroom without having nightmares. I got a new car because no matter how much I had my car cleaned, the blood stains would not leave. Every time I looked in the passenger seat, I saw him holding his face.

We moved to a house near my old high school. This was also a time when things started turning even worse. I got a second job, for insurance purposes and the extra money of course. Our relationship was falling apart. I started entertaining different guys on the phone to get my mind off my jacked-up relationship.

I went to a party at the Elks Club, with my first cousin Doug. We had a good time. We left there and went to the Huddle House. My boyfriend called me and asked where I was.

"Out." Is what I said to him. Someone had told him that they saw me in the truck with a man. Keep in mind, it was my cousin. He called me again and asked where I was. I told him, Huddle House. I had just got my daughter a new mustang for her sweet sixteen birthday. He jumped into her car and came to the Huddle House where we were. My cousin and I were sitting in his truck outside. My boyfriend pulls up and asks me to get out.

"Why?" I asked.

"Get out!"

"No!"

My cousin chimes in, "if she don't want to get out, she don't have to."

My boyfriend pulls a gun and demands, "Dee, get out now!"

My life flashed before my eyes. The thoughts of what had happened just a few months ago had me terrified. I knew anything could happen. My cousin also had a gun, but he did not pull it out.

My cousin goes on to say, "you can get out if you want to, but you don't have to." To keep the situation from escalating more I get out and get into the car with him. My door wasn't closed all the way before he drove off. It ended up hitting another car as he drove off. It messed up my daughter's passenger side door. My cousin chased us as we were speeding down Bluecutt Road. By this time, the police were called. And the chase ended.

We decided that we were not the best for each other, and I asked him to move out. He did without putting up a fight. We kept in touch, and he texted me every morning. It was always a motivational text, bible scriptures, or a simple "Have a good day." One morning I was getting ready for work to go to my second job. He texted, but I did not reply. He called back-to-back, but I did not answer. I knew how he was, so I figured he had ridden by my house. Suddenly, I heard a loud sound at my back door. He had broken into my house. He walked back to the room where I was and grabbed me by my hair. He beat me senselessly. The last thing I remember was waking up in the hospital. I used to be furious with my nosey neighbors. But if it weren't for them, I probably would have been dead. They saw when he kicked in my door and called the police. They thought someone was breaking into my house and that's why they called.

I was beat so bad my face was unrecognizable. I had a chipped tooth, black eyes, and concussion. My family and friends, but mostly my children, were so upset. They released me from the hospital and my parents both came and stayed the first night with me.

He was charged for what he did to me, but after we both talked,

I agreed to have the charges dropped. I couldn't. The state picked up the charges. I went up there a few months later to get them dropped, but they told me I could not and scared me into believing that if I dropped the charges I would get charged. At that time, I didn't know any better, so I never dropped the charges. We tried to fix our relationship, but it didn't work. I asked myself, "how can I be with someone who I am afraid of?" I blamed myself for all the things he did to me. I felt if I was a better woman, he would have loved me differently instead of trying to hurt me. I took the blame for everything that had happened to me thus far in my life. Now, it was time to put me FIRST.

By the age of twenty-six, I was in a rocky marriage. I had three beautiful children, owned a daycare center, nice car and house. everything I had dreamed of as a child I had. Seeing my mom struggle to take care of us gave me that go getter mentality. I made a promise to myself that my children would have everything I did not or could not have. And I lived up to that. They had cars, nice clothes, shoes, bedrooms. You name it. They had it. I felt like I was doing what I was supposed to be doing. But I was in a very unhappy place, and that's because I was taught to survive and work hard. Any man that came into my life and tried to be a real man to me I wouldn't let him. I was used to being the man and the woman of my household. I always had to hold things down, no matter who I was with. Being strong is weak when you are pretending. In life I learned at this point only those who care about you can still hear you when you are quiet and be a fountain not a drain.

Chapter *Ten*

I started working at SITEL, a call center, so that I could have some insurance, because standalone insurance was too expensive. I started off on the phones and worked my way up to team lead, then to forecasting. I loved SITEL, that is where I met half of the people I know now. There were a few that I absolutely loved; one was Tamara, she is from Crawford. I loved her spirit, and she was one of the prettiest young ladies ever. She always wore a smile. Anytime I needed someone to help the associates on the floor she would be my first pick every time. Another was Boomer, he was like my big/little brother. He was always the same every time I saw him. Then there was my homegirl Chandelier! She ended up moving to the same apartment complex as me. We have been friends ever since. Then, I met this guy who worked in my department, it was a rollercoaster. We dated for six years until I decided to move to Georgia. Things fell off with us, and we fell out of love. We had so much history, and stories that would last longer than the earth.

All my moms' grandchildren were very athletic, they had a league in the park where they played softball every summer. They were always selected to play in the All-Star league. They also played high school softball and fastpitch. With me owning my own business I could travel with them wherever they went. We were all over Mississippi playing ball. It was a fun time. This kept my mom happy; she looked forward to packing her coolers with drinks and snacks. Setting up tents to stay out of the sun. There was one incident when the high school coach had my baby girl Booty, on the high school team. I did not agree with it, because she was so young and not experience enough yet. The coach put her in to run for someone. She got out at home plate because she did not hear the coach tell her to stop at third base. The coach started fussing and cussing at her. I overheard her call her a tittie baby. That is when I lost it. The coach and I had words.

As my children were walking to get back onto the bus with their team, The coach shouted, "Don't get on my bus. Ride with your mom." I was glad that I drove my daycare van, because I had enough room for them to ride back with me and their belongings. The next day I went to the superintendent, and pleaded my case, about the incident. I sent emails to everyone on the board.

At the next meeting I was on the docket to stand before the board to plead my case. I was told that I was banned from the rest of the games for the season. I was furious, I never missed any of their games, I wasn't upset about her saying what she said to me. It was more about how she put my children off the bus. They were her responsibility. The next day after the board meeting, they fired her from the Head Softball/Fastpitch Coach. I was still not allowed to start going back to all the games. They were afraid I was going to sue the school. That's the only reason things went in my favor. They finished the school year with a new coach, Coach Jamie. She was the best and she respected the children. My childhood friends, and my sister's childhood friends, all had children, and they all played ball together. Michelle, Katrina, Vet, and Keisha, just to name a few. Their children Que, and Porsha were extremely good. They were hitting home runs every game. Que used to get so mad because soon as she came to bat, they would put her on base so that she wouldn't get a chance to hit. She was always hitting homeruns. They knew what she was going to do. Those babies didn't play around when it came to some ball.

I was now divorced. I closed the daycare down, and a little while after I decided to move to Georgia. I moved in with my cousin for about three months, I needed to make sure that's what I wanted to do before I made a commitment to stay there. I met a guy named, Gerald, before leaving Mississippi and moving my things to Georgia. My mom absolutely loved him. She would cook, and make sure he got a plate. He would do drop byes just to sit and talk to my mom. When she needed anything done, he was there. It was unbelievable how he treated her like a mother-in-law lol. My mom told me many times, "Dee that is your husband." She would tell all my family that also. Basically, anything my family needed; he was there. He attended my children's functions and helped when needed. He was one of a kind, never looked for anything in return. He and my son moved everything out of my townhouse to bring it to Georgia.

They had called me the day they were supposed to move my furniture and told me they couldn't find a U haul. I was furious because I had it set up for my things to arrive that day. Then, I heard a knock at the door. It was them. They got me. I immediately got happy. They started moving my things in and I cussed them out the entire time. They scratched my headboard as well as on a lot of my things. I was really just grateful that they made it safely.

Gerald would come to visit sometimes, I remember one time he came, and surprised me with my children, and sister for my birthday. He packed my family up and brought them to Atlanta to celebrate my birthday. When they walked in all I wanted to do was cry. I was in disbelief. He knew I had just moved there that April, and, I was lonely, missing my children. My cousin Monika knew and kept it a secret. They took me to the Cheesecake Factory for dinner and gave me gifts. We had a great time. I hated to see them leave.

It was Spring break, my sister "Christina" brought my nieces and nephew to Georgia. I was so excited to see them, because I rarely had anyone to really come visit me. Christina is the mother of my two nieces. We clicked instantly. We have had a bond since, forever. Always been supportive, and listens to all my ideas, dreams, and goals. When it was time for them to leave it broke my heart. But I knew they had to get back into their everyday life. Until this day, we are still connected, and we have each other's back. She's basically my self-care partner, sister, listening ear, but most of all, FRIEND.

It was the end of June 2014, my birthday weekend. Drico decided to come to Atlanta to celebrate his last few days of being single, before he got married in a few days. Boy, did we have time. He brought a few of his friends with him his brother EI, Josh, Quint, just to name a few, but it was like ten or twelve of them. I had a VIP section at DOA "Diamonds of Atlanta. We had a blast from the past. The next night we went to the U-Bar. In there they had this mechanical bull. I got up there and didn't last a minute without falling off. It was so much fun. We had a got a section, and we partied and had a good ole time. The next week Drico got married. A few months later we were talking and he said "Dee in going to open up a bar, in Columbus Ms. I was just listening to his idea, because he's always been smart, and a go-getter. The in 2018 he opened his first Sports Bar called the "YO BAR"

I was finally living comfortably. I was making good money, big, nice house living the lifestyle I always dreamed of. Traveling the world and making new memories. I met new friends, ate at different restaurants. I was taking my Granddaughter Jordynn and GOD baby Dyiamond on yearly trips. Disney World, Bahamas, Florida, Cruises, just to name a few. I wanted them to see the world at a young age. My son Christopher excelled in school and sports. He landed his first job at Kroger and became a front-end manager at the age of sixteen. He had a nice car, living good, buying what he wanted. He and I would have a date night every weekend. We would just get into the car and ride around until we were lost, just to see new areas. We would try different restaurants, and foods. We would go to games. Things were looking good for me. I was finally stress free and moving forward. I would go home maybe once a month to visit my mom and see a few friends. Then back on the highway back to Georgia I would go.

It was Chris, my baby and only son's eighteenth birthday. I had us shirts made for his big day. I told him on the morning of his birthday to pack a bag. He had no idea what I had planned. He was like, "mom it's my 18th birthday I want to thang with my friends."

I said, "you can, when we get back."

We pulled up at the airport. His eyes got big, and he said, "mom, are we fixing to fly? My first flight really?"

I said, "Yes son, anything to make your day special."

We got to luggage drop off, he still had no idea where we were going. Finally, they said "all passengers boarding for a flight to Miami Florida, please line up here when your section is called."

He said, "mom, are you taking me to Miami for my birthday."

"Yes, I am."

He had the time of his life, I took him to the finest Steak House, for his birthday dinner. He rented a jet ski every day. It was all about him. My baby was not a baby anymore.

It was his senior year and he wanted to attend school back in Mississippi. The main reason was that he wouldn't have to pay out of state tuition for college. The second reason was so he could graduate with his friends. He ended up moving to Starkville with my best friend LaToya the second semester of his senior year. She took loving care of him and made sure he had everything he needed.

Chapter *Eleven*

The was another guy who gave me the world, his name was Rodney. The only downside was I didn't see him a lot because he stayed on the road. When I say he stayed on the road a lot, I mean a lot. When he did come home, he would wine and dine me. With all of this, the love wasn't there. Maybe the love wasn't there because all we did was talk on the phone for the most part of our relationship. Seems like he would rather work than be home. I just went along with it. During this time Social media was hot, so anytime I posted anything, guys even women would get into my inbox. I love to travel. I had a team who was just like me, Monika, Wendy, and I would jump and go with quickness. Whatever I said I wanted to do for my birthday we did it, lol. My friends were down for whatever adventure I planned. For this particular birthday we planned a trip to Miami.

My best friend Toya, her sister Ty, Kim, Sheena, Christina, Monika, Wendy, and I rented a truck and went. We had a blast. It was my thirty eighth birthday and it was a trip well needed. Anyway, we took photos on the beach, and I posted away. A guy named Bubba commented on one of the pics that I posted. So, the first thing I do is go to his page and scroll through his pictures to see what he does for a living. After I finished my screening, I hit him back with thanks handsome. He was strong, hard-working, handsome, and

BIPOLAR Lol!

I was dating someone at the time but, it was on its last leg, so I started talking with Bubba. We started off as friends only and we would talk here and there. Nothing major. I felt like he wasn't my type … at first. Then, he invited me on a trip. I was like, "hmm this man don't know if I'm a man or woman and he wants to take me on a trip." So, I agreed. This was like about five months later after we became friends. Let's just say that after that trip I was hooked. That's crazy coming from me because it took a lot for me to ever say something like this. That man could touch me, and I would melt. He was romantic and knew how to cater to a lady. We started learning each other, and decided to became a couple.

Have you ever met a person who completed you? A person who could just touch you and it felt like the first time EVERY time? A person that can make you laugh, and mad at the same time. A person that can take a city girl and turn them into a country girl? Yea, that feeling, butterflies and all. He understands me and encourages me when I'm down. We bumped heads, but we loved each other. We can party together, drink, laugh, travel, work, cook, you name it together. I felt like he completed me. Once I took him to Cancun for his birthday. The resort was breathtaking. We have a jacuzzi tub out on the balcony. Boy did we have time in there lol. We stayed for four days. My daughter Booty was pregnant and due at the end of the month so, I had no worries about her going in labor while I was on vacation. I was able to relax.

On our third day there we did excursions. One of the

excursions had us climb up these stairs, grab a rope, and dump off into the lake. Bubba didn't want to do it but, "me being a damn fool" decided to take the challenge. I was scared as hell. Some of the people with us were cheering me on saying "you can do it." There were lifeguards waiting in the lake as you let go of the rope, but I was still scared as hell. It was finally my turn to go. I had on a life jacket. I had wrapped my braids up because they were long. I grabbed the rope, and they pushed me off the edge. I panicked! As, I was swinging to the lake I kept telling myself, "Dee let the rope go." If I didn't, I would go straight into the woods and probably kill myself. I let go. There was a lake full of people along with three lifeguards. I went to what seemed like to be the bottom of the lake. My braids came down and some were in my mouth. I was choking from the water and braids that had gotten into my mouth. The next thing I knew the lifeguards were coming to help me. I had on a life jacket and was acting like I was drowning! They finally got me to the stairs to get back to the top where Bubba was waiting. Tell me why he was crying tears laughing at me. He joked me and said "Dee why you lied like you could swim." I was so mad at him. From time to time he would joke with me, and to this day it's funny as I look back on it. You would have to be there to understand how funny that was.

It was our last day there and we were about to head to the airport, and I got a call saying "Booty in the hospital she in labor" I was furious! I wanted to be there. We boarded the plane and that was the last time I could talk to her because we would be in the air.

For two hours we were in the air. I was praying she would hold on until I got there but, when we landed my grandbaby was born. I was so disappointed, but I knew that was out of my control.

Chapter *Twelve*

My mom started being sick more often. She went to the doctor and told us that the doctor told her something that she wasn't going to share with us. I was furious, because I wanted to know. She never told me. She would always say when she was mad or frustrated that we were going to miss her when she gone. Until this day I still hate those words. I started coming home every weekend due to him being sick more than usual.

I had this guy friend that I met. We started off as friends, then as time passed, we became a couple. If you know me, you know my birthday is a major holiday for me, lol. I would always go out of the country every year and evert five years have a party. It was my fortieth birthday party; I came home to have an all-white birthday party. Things didn't go how I planned but I really enjoyed myself. The next day my friends and I flew out to Vegas, Wendy, Monika and Priscilla. This was a special trip because we were celebrating my fortieth birthday, and for the second, it was Wendy and Priscilla's first flight. I was honored that they put their fears aside and flew with me for my birthday.

Before I could turn forty-two, my mom and dad were both ill; My dad had back-to-back strokes some months prior, and a slight heart attack. He was a strong man. I was at Disney World with my granddaughter and GOD child. My sister Narquita called me first and said, "Dee, dad sick, and they are admitting him in the hospital." I told my babies that we had to cut our trip short, even though we had three days left. We had already been there three days. I got our new flight details, and we flew back to Georgia the next day. We stayed at home that night and drove to Mississippi the next morning. I went straight to the hospital to see my dad.

When I got to the hospital, I stopped by the nurse's station to get his room number. Once I got the number, I went down the hall to his room. As I walked into the room, I saw a body lying there, I thought I was in the wrong room, so I immediately turned around. I went back to the nurse's station and asked again to make sure I had the right room. Once again, she gave me the number and walked me to the room. I was in total disbelief. That was not my dad that was lying there! His eye was swollen due to the fluid buildup. He looked totally different. He was not the man I looked at for forty-one years. Tears began to fall, I was speechless. The nurse gave me a hug and told me it would be alright.

I told her, "No it won't. do you see him?"

I knew my dad was transitioning to leave us. My sister called and said she was on her way back up there. We sat with my dad for a while and tried to talk to him. His speech was not good due to his sickness. We left to handle some business for him. When we got back the doctor came in to let us know what the next steps would be. His body was rejecting the medicine, and there was basically nothing left they could do for him.

The next day, my dad's best friend Donnie, came in and we

talked. He told me that he was going to bring his clippers and cut my dad's hair. My dad didn't like to be out of place. That's where I got it from. Donnie goes on to say, "Dee, he good. He told me he had got right with GOD, and that he was ready to go."

Tears wouldn't stop, but a sense of relief came over my body. We all fall short of HIS Glory. Just to know he repented and, told his best friend he got right with GOD, helped me to forgive him for some of the things he did to me as a child. I silently said, "I forgive you." That Wednesday evening my dad needed a charger to charge his phone so that he could get some information out of it. My mom came up to the hospital where we were and brought one for him. She looked at my dad, and I could see in her eyes she knew it wouldn't be long until he was gone.

She asked about him daily. I jokingly said to her once "I see you worried about your husband." just to make her laugh. She cussed me out, and we laughed. She went home, and I went back to Bubba's house to rest. A week later, which was the following Wednesday, my sister Kita called and said that mom was sick. She told mom that if she didn't let her take her to the hospital, she was going to call the ambulance. My mom finally got dressed and went to the emergency room. Now, my mom and dad were both at Baptist Memorial Hospital, in Columbus, Mississippi. Once they got my mom back to the room, they ran different tests. Then, as I was sitting in the chair waiting on the Doctor to come in, I looked up and it was Doctor Manning. She was the same Doctor that came in and, announced my sister Monique's death, exactly eighteen years ago. I was in disbelief. For one I was astonished to see that she was still there after eighteen years, and for two she was the person that came bearing bad news.

I immediately said, "Hi Dr, Manning, do you remember us?"

"Yes, I remember all of you."

At that moment my heart dropped.

She asked how we all had been doing and we all said, "fine." She then went on to say to my mom, "Mrs. Ledbetter your kidneys are shutting down. We will have to contact your doctor and see what he would like to do next."

My mom broke down, and said, "she messed me up! That lady messed me up!"

My mom had gone to a doctor's appointment a few weeks prior. Her original doctor was out when she went. They had a nurse practitioner to see her, and she messed up her dosage of medication. It was too strong, and it started dehydrating her kidneys. My mom then asked for the phone so she could call her good friend Elnora. Elnora's daughter Rochelle answered the phone and when asked, she stated that Elnora wasn't home. My mom broke down crying.

That tore me up inside. I went up the second floor to let my dad know that mom was downstairs in the emergency room. He couldn't talk. His words were slurred, but he got so upset. He started kicking and making sounds. It was his way of letting us know he was upset and wanted to know what was going on. He finally calmed down so that I could tell him she would be ok. I went back downstairs to where my mother was. At this point Dr. Manning was back and she said that my mom's heart doctor requested that she comes to Tupelo to be monitored more closely. My mom started crying again. I just stopped and stared at her. She didn't look sick, she looked like her normal self. She always would feel bad every now and then, but never bad down sick. She was so strong, and barely showed signs of weakness. The ambulance took my mom to Tupelo to get admitted so that her doctor could monitor her properly.

I was beyond stressed at this point. My dad was in Columbus, my mom was in Tupelo, and it was exactly one week until my son walked across the stage to graduate. My boyfriend was off working. I had this big ass house in Georgia that I had just recently got not even a year prior. My job and everything else were at stake at this point. My anxiety went through the roof, stress level was extremely high, life was getting the best of me.

For a week straight my family and I were back and forth between hospitals. We moved from couch to couch, we were all so exhausted. It was May 10, 2017, at exactly 5:07 A. M. I woke up on the couch in my mom's room. I said, "mom, I will be back later, when I take a shower, go see dad, and get some rest."

She didn't reply.

I said, "woman you hear me?" because I always joke with her like that.

She then said, "Okay, Dee."

I walked out and went home to shower. I got a call around half past twelve that afternoon. They had me on speaker phone. The doctor was in the room and a few family members. *My mom had told me a few days earlier that they suggested that she go on the machine.* Then she goes to say, "Dee they want to put me in ICU."

I got quiet.

Then she said, "Dee you there?"

I said "yes."

The doctor went into his spill about her blood pressure dropping too low, and a few other things. I asked, "what do you want to do mom?"

She said, "Dee I just want to get well and go home."

Those were the last words she said to me. The look on her face now, when I think back, was a look of fear, she hadn't wanted me to leave that day. I question myself all of the time. Why didn't' I notice the sign? Why didn't I stay? Why didn't I ask more questions? Why didn't I know?" I never knew my mom was telling me that she was ready to go home, to be with the LORD.

My thoughts from that day forward were to heal the root, so that the tree remains stable.

My oldest daughter Ta'Dashea came home and stayed with my mom. Every time that machine would go off, she would go over to my mom and tell her to breathe. She was on it, making sure my mom didn't give up. On that following Tuesday, the hospice told my sister Narquita, that my dad wouldn't make it through the night. At that time the hospice was in the hospital instead of the nursing home. That Wednesday morning, he was still alive.

The first call I got was from my cousin Eddie. He told me that my dad had passed. I was on the highway coming from Jackson, when I got the call. No one wanted me to know while I was driving on the highway. The second call was from one of my best friends, LaToya, then my best friend Wendy. They both were concerned about me driving that far. So, Wendy told me to meet her in Starkville in Walmart parking lot. I did and she drove me over to the hospital to release my dad's body.

When I got there to the hospital, family and friends were there. When I was walking through the door my niece Olivia was screaming and crying. I walked in and headed to the elevator. Drico, whispered into my ear, "it's true." I acted as if I didn't hear him. Then suddenly, I seen my cousin Tracy with my sister, I immediately broke down. All I remember is us hitting the floor. We finally made it upstairs to my dad's floor. Once I got there my oldest daughter grabbed and hugged me. She broke down, so I had to stay strong, because that's what my dad taught me. Never show signs of weakness. I feel like that's why I'm so damaged now. I then walked into the room. My eyes were glued on my dad, the man that helped to bring me into this world. The man that raised me. The first man I ever loved. He was the man that taught me how to drive, how to clean a house from top to bottom, how to remain strong in any situation. He was gone, in the flesh, but not in spirit.

My phone rang, and I snapped out of it. At that very moment what Drico had whispered in my ear was true. I told my family and friends, "Get in your cars, drive safely to Tupelo. We can go together and tell mom." I knew the entire time my mom was already gone. I just didn't let them know. There was no way that I could let them get on the highway knowing what to expect once they got there. The entire ride there I was in disbelief thinking it was a dream. Or was it a nightmare I couldn't wake up from.

My niece Tierra was already there with mom. She had been there all day with her, basically by herself. We finally pulled up. CeCe the nurse that was taking care of my mom, looked at me and asked, "are you, Dee?"

I said, "yes."

"Can I talk to you for a second?"

"Yes," as I walked with her.

She then went to say, "I walked in your moms' rooms; she woke up when I walked in. She said, 'this is the best sleep I've ever had.' When she said that she looked so peaceful and laid her head back."

Cece then goes to say, "I walked out of the room, and she coded. Dee she is at peace."

I lost it at that moment. Not my mom! She wasn't that sick! Why her? She's a good person. She will give you her last and do anything for anyone. She didn't smoke, drink, club, or anything. Why? When I walked into the room a lot of my family and friends were standing there surrounding her bed. My mom laid there with her head tilted a little to the left, with her mouth slightly opened like she was sleeping. All I saw at that moment was my sister Monique lying on the ground in the same position except her eyes were opened. We all bowed our heads in prayer and prayed over my mom's lifeless body.

Once we left the ICU room, we gathered in the parking lot

talking about how we couldn't believe what had just happened. They both passed on the same day. Exactly three hours and one minute apart. It sounded unbelievable. Then, it clicked in my head they got married March 1, 1974. The exact same numbers 3-1. They had been separated for over twenty-five years or so, but still legally married. They cared for each other even though they acted as if they couldn't stand each other. If my dad was hungry, she would feed him. If my mom needed some extra money, he gave it to her. That's love even though they couldn't be together.

My dad and mom always used to say, "We are not getting a divorce." If something happened to my dad before my mom, he wanted her to get his VA benefits. But their love was so strong, and unique they left together. That's the love I want to experience one day. People often ask me, "You mom must not have been able to take your dad leaving so she went too." I couldn't answer that, because for one we never got a chance to tell my mom he had passed. I don't know if she felt it in her heart and knew.

My aunt Nancy and I were talking, and I said, "I didn't know mom was that sick to die."

She told me "Dee I knew she was about to go; I could see it in her eyes."

That tore me apart because I was her daughter, her oldest child, and I didn't see it. I didn't have a clue. I thought she would get well and come home. But I was completely wrong. She left us to be with my dad and sister.

Protect your energy, at all costs, because this is when the enemy tried to come in a destroy my family. Wednesday, May 10, 2017, I lost the two people who gave me life, and brought me into this world. They were gone, taken away from us.

It left me speechless. What was I supposed to do? I couldn't do this. How was I supposed to do this? I don't have the strength, nor the will power. LORD what am I supposed to do? That following Sunday was Mother's Day. I was bitter, angry, sad, mad and jealous because the people that surrounded me had their mother. I lost mine four days ago. What did I do that was so bad to deserve this? Was this payback for my wrong doings? I'm such a bad person that my parents had to be taken from me. WHY? WHY? I needed answers. We all decided to go to my sister's church that morning, New Beginnings. The service was beautiful and what we all needed, they prayed for us and let us know we would stay in their prayers. They were very helpful during our time of need.

Chapter *Thirteen*

The following days ahead was torture. Getting my mom's house together and the funeral arrangements had my mind all over the place. I was still in disbelief about what was going on. The love and support were remarkable. My best friends were there for me like no other. Toya who has been like a backbone to me and my children, prayed for me and with me. She gave me reassurance that HE wouldn't put more on me than I can bare. Bubba was on the boat, and was coming in the following week, He helped me keep sane, even when I felt like giving up. Wendy came after work every day no matter how tired she was, or what she had going on. Wendy even hosted a kickball tournament to help with the cost of the arrangements.

Priscilla came every morning as soon as she finished her bus route. She would come to cook and clean. She would then leave, and do her evening bus route, and come right back afterwards to cook and clean. She was literally my backbone. She wouldn't let me do anything. Her sister Teka cooked us gourmet meals daily without hesitation. Drico was supportive as well, he gave me talks, and told me I had to be strong for their family. He came by every day to help keep our spirits up. And, if you know LIEDRICO as he calls himself you know he kept us laughing.

My cousin Monika made me get out of my comfort zone. I have

a lot of pride, and I never asked a soul for anything. She called me and told me, "Dee I can't get to you until Friday, but I'm coming. Hold on until I get there." I broke down, because she knows me better than anyone. And, to hear her say that let me know my circle was complete. I knew then that I had the right people I needed to help me get through one of the toughest times in my life.

Having the right people in your life is so important. Not just in grief, but in the good times too. So, many people, too many to name Blessed us with food, drinks, money, cash apps, cards, flowers, encourage words, visits, and most importantly prayers. I could never with a million tongues thank them enough.

I asked the Pastor at a bigger church, not the one my parents belong to but, another one, because it was bigger and, I knew it would be big enough to host the funeral. I was immediately directed to contact their home church Pastor because it was his call. At first, I was furious then it was explained to me by others, whatever he says goes. I contacted him and set up a meeting. All I could think about as I walked into my home church, the church I grew up in, the church that my membership was at, and the church where my grandmother and aunts and uncles' funerals had been, was anger.

I immediately thought back to when we met with the Pastor about my sister. I had a feeling it wasn't going to go smoothly; I whispered a little prayer, walked in and we had our meeting. This went great. We talked and figured things out. He agreed to have the funeral at the church I selected, if the Pastor agreed. Now, we had to find clothing for my mom and dad. We came up with purple and gray. My mom's favorite color was purple, so that's why that color was picked. Most of my dad's suits were gray, so that's why we chose gray. The girls in the family wore purple dresses with a gray rose, and the guys wore gray suits with a purple rose.

Then the hardest part came when it was time to do the obituaries. Josh, who worked at Carters where my mom and dad's bodies were, had helped us through the motions of everything. He was there every step of the way. My mother and father did not have insurance. My mom and I had just talked about insurance in January of that year. She told me she was going to get some. I was under the impression my dad had some through VA since he was getting the benefits. I was beyond stressed, some family on both sides and mostly friends helped us out tremendously. Their church home helped as well. The only thing I had was my 401k. I did what I had to do to make sure my parents were buried properly. I didn't want to owe anyone, or a bank. That money was in there for a reason and that was the reason.

Some of the family was upset because we decided to have a double funeral. At a time like this I had family in my ear about burying them together. First off, I'm grieving, my sister, children, nieces, nephews are grieving. Secondly, they were still legally married, but they had been separated for over twenty-five years and they still cared for each other. Third, there wasn't any way on GOD green earth that I would take my family through two separate funerals.

I had no clue as to what to write in the obituaries. My mom and dad had so many outside sisters and brothers as, they call them. I didn't want to leave anyone out. My cousin Stephanie and Toya let me use my aunt Linda's obituary to help with my dad's side. Since I was doing a double obituary. I thought I had everything perfect for his side, only to find out that I left my aunt Linda name out of his obituary. That really crushed my heart. I didn't even realize it until my cousin told me. I still beat myself up about that to this day.

On my mom's side of the obituary My aunt Nancy, and aunt Mary helped me. It was a beautiful double folded obituary of both my parents. The pallbearers were the hardest part. Everyone loved my mom and dad. We made our finial decisions and went with what we thought was best.

That day before the funeral we had to go early to view the bodies. Me and my family walked in, I wasn't prepared to see what I was about to see. I was sick to my stomach. I had so much hate and rage in my heart. I was blunt with my words, harsh with my feelings, and numb to life. *Only those who care about you can still hear you when you are quiet.*

My stomach was in knots. I didn't want to see my mom and dad laying lifeless in a casket. I didn't want to accept that these were the final days of me seeing them in the flesh. But I had to remind myself, "if you are sure to live, you are sure to die."

We went in and I went to my mom first. She looked as if she was asleep. She looked exactly how she always looked. They made her look alive. A few hours later family and friends gathered together for the wake. People came from everywhere. There wasn't enough room for the everyone to sit. People were saying prayers, giving hugs, speaking life into our family, giving love offerings, and giving their condolences. We gathered back at my mom's house to meet with family and get my mom's house together.

The house my mom was renting belonged to a man that had a car lot on 82 in east Columbus. He had absolutely no sympathy at all, so we had to do things quickly, after everything was over. We laughed, cried, and had a good time that night, as we prepared ourselves for the next day.

Later that night, I got sick, I was throwing up, lightheaded, mad, and hurt. All I could think about was, "I'm burying my mother AND father in the morning." My son, my baby was about to walk across the stage to graduate. I finally went to sleep around three that morning only to be back up six. I could not sleep for nothing; I tossed and turned all night.

Finally, that morning came, I was numb. I talked to Bubba, and he assured me everything was going to be ok. I heard the words, but I didn't feel them. I got to my mom's house, that's where we lined up to go to the church. We had two family cars, one for my mom's side and one for my dad's side. Both cars were full. I told Josh that I would just drive, because there wasn't any more room. He insisted, "No Dee, we will make it work." So, I sat in the front seat on the way to the church. When we pulled up to the church there were people everywhere. Some of my dad's family, I hadn't seen before, came to the car when we pulled up to check on us. Finally, the time came for us to get out of the car and walk in the church. When they opened my door, my heart dropped. I got out, we all gathered, and we walked in the church. So, so, many people were there. As I looked forward, I seen my mom's and dad's caskets. I went blank after that. The next thing I remember was when they were closing the caskets and laid my dad's flag across his casket. It felt like I couldn't breathe.

The service started, my son Christopher grabbed my hand and held me the entire time without letting go. I looked back and seen family and so many of my friends there in support. That's when I lost it, LORD HAVE MERCY on me LORD, help me! One of my mom's best friends Linda, got up to speak, everything she said was so true, my mom loved that woman. Linda was what you called a real friend. Even when they stopped working together, they always kept in touch. The pastor was preaching I heard a loud thumb! I was scared to turn around, but later I found out what that thumb was. *That Doug and Drico need JESUS, let's just say that.* As we walked out to get back in the car to go to the burial site. Reality kicked in. I really wasn't going to see my parents anymore. They were really gone.

I Am a Survivor!

I AM a rape survivor.

I AM a domestic violence survivor.

I AM a survivor of witnessing my boyfriend shoot himself in front of me.

I AM a survivor of watching my sister take her last breath in my arms.

I AM a survivor of losing both of my parents on the same day.

I AM a survivor of being a single/black mother of three

I AM a survivor of physical and emotional abuse.

I AM a survivor of being treated differently/mistreated by family members.

I AM a survivor of being broke.

I AM a survivor of Not being chosen.

I AM a survivor of Generational Curses.

I AM a survivor of family secrets.

I AM a survivor of lies and greed.

I AM a survivor of brokenness.

I AM a survivor of hate.

I AM a survivor of being cheated on.

I AM a survivor of being left out.

I AM a survivor of adultery.

I AM a survivor of my own mind.

I AM a survivor of attempted suicide.

I AM A SURVIVIOR BECAUSE I SURVIVED TO TELL MY STORY.

Deneatrice Ledbetter

www.ingramcontent.com/pod-product-compliance
Lightning Source LLC
Chambersburg PA
CBHW031219120626
46545CB00003B/906